04/10/15

WITHDRAWN
11/4/23 SM

The 20 British Prime Ministers
of the 20th century

This book is dedicated to the citizens of Rotherham with thanks for allowing me to serve in our Parliament and sit in the Commons, a privilege and honour given to few and which made my mother who died in 2006 immensely proud and would have made my father, wounded fighting fascism in the Second World War, equally proud had he not died in 1958.

Heath

RT. HON. DENIS MACSHANE MP

HAUS PUBLISHING • LONDON

First published in Great Britain in 2006 by
Haus Publishing Limited
26 Cadogan Court
Draycott Avenue
London SW3 3BX

www.hauspublishing.co.uk

A CIP catalogue record for this book is available from the British Library

ISBN 1-904950-69-8

Designed by BrillDesign
Typeset in Garamond 3 by MacGuru Ltd
info@macguru.org.uk

Printed and bound by Graphicom, Vicenza

Front cover: John Holder

Contents

Foreword

Why is a Labour MP writing a biography of Edward Heath? The custom is for political biographers to have some empathy with, or indeed be of the same broad political family as, their subject. It is unlikely that the kind of feel that some of our finest political biographers have for their subjects – think Ben Pimlott on Dalton, Simon Heffer on Powell, Alan Bullock on Bevin, Michael Foot on Bevan, or Susan Crosland on Crosland – would be there if they had to write about leaders and former ministers across the political divide. My connection with Edward Heath is limited. When I made my maiden speech as an MP after winning a by-election for the seat of Rotherham in 1994 I did so in a debate on Europe. Heath spoke in the same debate. We left the Chamber together. 'Good speech,' he grunted. He was not up for much communication. I joined the Labour Party in 1970 in response to decisions Edward Heath took as Prime Minister. My first period as a trade union activist and Labour Party officer, and then parliamentary candidate in 1974 took place under Heath. I spent the 1980s working abroad and did not see close up what has been fairly described as the 'longest sulk in history'. But when I became an MP, my view of Heath changed. He stood like some limpet-covered rock cut off from the safe shore of the Thatcher-Major Conservative party against which the thundering waves of Euroscepticism crashed with no discernible impact. He was above all a Parliamentarian. All MPs enter the Commons with the hope of a red box, and even the key to Number 10 in the bag. Once they have achieved that aim, most cannot wait to get out of the Commons with its obligations to vote at all hours, and constituents demanding attention around the clock. Heath spent more time as backbencher than he did as a minister. He took Parliament seriously and it seems appropriate that an MP should essay a narrative of his life. In my maiden speech in 1994, I referred to Ted Heath's opposition to the appeasement policies of the Conservatives in the 1930s. His maiden speech made 44 years previously was an appeal for Britain to be serious about European construction. He had less than four years in the high office of Prime Minister but in that period he took one momentous decision that will give him a place in history – namely Britain joined the European Economic Community and has been part of the European Community, now the European Union ever since. That decision had and has the most profound impact on our island life. So I hope readers will accept that I, also a keen Parliamentarian, and a strong pro-European in British public life, have some credentials to attempt a life of Heath. The early years of the 21st century when I served as Minister for Europe are not the same at the early 1960s or when Heath took Britain into Europe in 1972. But the ways of Whitehall, and the arguments behind the scenes over Europe, are not so very different. I have been able to talk to Conservative MPs who worked with him. None have given me a special insight. There was an 'unknown unknown', to use a later phrase, about Heath that went to the grave with him. This short book, in addition to presenting to the general reader a life of Heath, is in part a commentary on the politics with a small 'p' of Parliament and Government as seen from the inside. Heath's successes and failures belong to any political lexicon at any time. Heath was a prime minister who changed Britain forever but was unable to change himself.

I would like to thank the House of Commons Library, Nur Laiq and David Young for their help with research.

Part One

THE LIFE

Chapter 1: Early Years

Edward Heath was born in east Kent on 9 July 1916 in the middle of the Somme offensive and in the same year as Harold Wilson and François Mitterrand. Responding to Europe's long civil war between 1914 and 1945 by ensuring that such barbarity could never happen again was the leitmotif in Heath's political life. English popular history sees only the fighting between 1914 and 1918 and 1939 and 1945, yet there was not a day of full peace in Europe for the three decades between the summer of 1914 and the spring of 1945. And even if soldiers were not firing shots, there was the grim oppression of authoritarian regimes of the left and right denying basic rights to millions of Europeans. Another theme in Heath's life was resistance to socialism and he and Harold Wilson were locked in direct political combat for a decade. Wilson emerged the winner in terms of elections won but it was Heath who had the bigger historic impact by taking Britain into Europe. And shortly after both men left high office, the politics of Britain was fundamentally reshaped by the arrival of a new hard neo-liberal Toryism which became known as Thatcherism, which, in turn, gave birth to New Labour. Finally, Heath's life was intimately bound up with France. All British politicians are divided between those who are romantic about France, like Churchill, Macmillan and Heath, and those petty Francophobes who find France irritating and ever in the way of English desires and designs. Heath's private walk with the French president Pompidou in the gardens of the Elysée in 1972 allowed the breakthrough to let the United Kingdom join the European Community.

Making Europe safe from conflict. Arguing against statist socialism. Seeking a rapprochement with France. These three themes wove their way through Edward Heath's life. He came from modest origins. His father was a hands-on builder and carpenter who put in 16-hour days six days a week. Harold Wilson's biographer, Ben Pimlott, contrasted the 'northern lower-middle-class' roots of Wilson's parents compared to 'Harold's later opponent, and Oxford contemporary, Edward Heath, whose manual working-class roots are indisputable'[1] but Heath's own biographer John Campbell says Heath was 'born into the upwardly mobile, socially aspiring skilled working class just where it merges into the lower middle class'.[2] The writhing of British historians and sociologists about the divisions and frontiers of the country's class system and where exactly to locate each Briton has been a 20th-century obsession and the object of satire by observant comedians like John Cleese and Ronnie Corbett. What is clear is that Heath was 100 per cent English. Kent is the garden of England. Its coast running from Dover up the Thames estuary is not the same as the fields and woods where Churchill bought his country house, Chartwell, or where the British Foreign Secretary has a handsome Jacobean house at Chevening. The Kent coast is a hard-working region. There were coal mines just 20 miles from Broadstairs, Heath's home town. The Medway towns, Sittingbourne, Chatham, Dartford and Sheerness are towns where manual employees co-exist with the service and professional middle classes. Broadstairs, Ramsgate and Margate were holiday towns for Londoners on modest incomes. Whichever party wins this part of England usually forms a government. Heath later adopted the costume and habits of the ruling Conservative class, but his roots were not theirs. His mother had the strong-faced beauty of a Julia Roberts to judge from photographs. Heath was extremely close to her and she did everything to protect and promote her son. In the summer, the family took in boarders, giving up rooms in their small house for paying guests to supplement household income. The family was never poor but Heath could not go to Oxford without a council scholarship and support from an educational charity. His parents were protective of him and his brother John who was four years younger. Like all small boys he was sent off to learn the piano but unlike most small boys the playing of music gripped him and swept Teddy, as he was called, into a world where his fingers and ears could make it his own. To master an instrument and become fully musical requires a kind of celibacy, a monastic discipline to surrender part of oneself to the art and craft of music. As other teenagers were out chasing girls, larking about or sneaking into pubs under-age, Heath was hunched over the piano and then the organ learning to play as if his future depended on it.

His other passion was reading. He had few friends. His sports were swimming and cycling, not team sport although he was scorer to the First Eleven – the job given to the school swot or weed who cannot be trusted with bat or ball. He won a scholarship to Chatham House, a grammar school in Ramsgate and became a prefect – the English system of turning boys into whips – at the age of 16. There was something puritanical, priggish and tightly focused about Heath. He wanted to do his school certificate – the equivalent today of GCSEs – at the age of 14 and persuaded his father to appeal to the school head to drop his objections to Heath taking the exam so young. Not keen on sport, Heath became a chorister and organ player at the local church. But he did like debates and spoke in a school debate that repeated the famous 1933 Oxford Union motion that 'this House would fight for King and Country.' Heath spoke in favour of fighting for ones country and unlike the pacifist neutralists at Oxford, Heath's team won a majority for the motion. *I suppose I just liked arguing*,[3] he wrote in order to explain this desire to take part in and win debates. Heath kept a home at his father's house in Broadstairs until the end of the 1960s. There he was completely at ease meeting childhood friends and in due course learning to sail. It was the most secure part of his life.

Like Neil Kinnock, Heath was the first member of his family to go to university. He set his heart on going to Oxford. Leaving the confined horizons of Broadstairs and the north Kent shoreline was important. As with so many, Oxford was the catalyst to a rebirth and an injection of confidence and a sense that anything can be achieved. He tried first for Keble, that dull redbrick Oxford Movement college dumped in the 19th century on the outskirts of the university town, but was turned down. But it was a blessing in disguise as Heath won a place at Balliol, a college where politics and appreciation of hard serious work went hand in hand. After a term he won an organ scholarship which required playing each morning in the college chapel. Harold Wilson never met his contemporary Edward Heath at Oxford but he did go to hear Heath playing the organ in the chapel at Balliol. If the Anglican Church was the Tory Party at prayer, playing the church's music each morning in Balliol was to live in a stable, ordered world as an undergraduate.

In his autobiography, Heath writes about his time at Oxford, which thanks to his music scholarship stretched to four years, not the usual three, with tenderness, yearning and detailed interest in all he did and all he met. For Heath,

Balliol, the starting point for so many in British public life, *provided a breadth of human experience, and understanding that I had never previously experienced. The College was also rightly renowned for its emphasis on public service, tolerance and intellectual integrity.*[4] Unlike so many of his contemporaries – Roy Jenkins, the student communist Denis Healey, or Anthony Crosland – Heath was not tempted towards the fashionable leftism of the student 1930s. On the contrary, he rose to head the university Conservative Association and became President of the Union. There already the Heath of the 1970s was evident as he called in a firm of management consultants from London and reorganised the union so that it offering food and other facilities in order to increase membership.

Heath's Oxford, with its focus on Oxford Union politics, was different from that of his contemporary, Harold Wilson. The northern boy was a swot, working 14 hours a day to get a first at the Welsh college, Jesus. He never went to the Union and although Wilson was to become a better House of Commons debater than Heath, his speaking powers were developed later. Heath was taught to marshal arguments and learnt to speak well and then went into politics, while Wilson was an intellectual – a university don while Heath was still an undergraduate – who learnt to speak after he was elected to the Commons. Success in Oxford undergraduate politics and its debating society, the Oxford Union, is little guide to future political ability. The quick-witted repartee that wins votes in the Oxford Union debates seduces those who have the gift of talking well into thinking that is all that is required for a political career. Wilson said nothing of note at Oxford but survived longer in Downing Street than his contemporary.

Clearly, at Oxford Heath gained the confidence to know that he could lead people, run institutions and effect change.

But perhaps the most important part of his four student years were spent not at the university but on trips abroad. Political tourism is now fashionable but there can be few post-war European leaders – an exception might be Willy Brandt – who saw first-hand the shape of European politics in the 1930s to the extent that Heath did. Heath was in Spain during the Civil War where he met Jack Jones, a young trade unionist from Liverpool who was in the International Brigades. He was at Nuremberg for the Nazi rallies and shook hands with Göring and Himmler, recalling the weak, clammy hand of the SS leader. In August 1939, Heath was in Danzig being urged to quit Poland by the British ambassador before the war started. He took in the music festival at Salzburg and hitch-hiked his way across France, picking up a knowledge of wine that never left him. If he mastered music, he had trouble with foreign languages. No linguist like Denis Healey he worked hard at his French and German. Much scorned for his strong English accent when he spoke in French at the moment of Britain joining the European Community, it remains no bad thing that from time to time there is a Prime Minister who can read more than his or her own language.

These vivid holidays spent in the political front-line of a Europe fighting to save democracy from Francoism or Hitlerism or Mussolini's buffoonish but murderous adventures in Africa were as important as the eight weeks he spent three times a year in Oxford. It meant that Heath's Conservatism turned quickly to that of Churchill's resistance of the appeasement of dictators which was the policy of Baldwin and Chamberlain in the 1930s just as it was the policy of a Conservative Prime Minister and Foreign Secretary in relation to Serbia and Rwanda in the 1990s. Heath was also attracted to the 'Middle Way' theories of Harold Macmillan, whose book of that name stunned his party and his class by arguing for a planned approach to economic development along the lines of Roosevelt's New Deal and based on the theories of John Maynard Keynes. Macmillan attacked the Conservatives as 'a party dominated by … company promoters – a Casino Capitalism – that is not likely to represent anything but itself'.[5]

He supported the Master of Balliol, Alexander Lindsay, in the 1938 by-election for the university seat when Lindsay stood as an anti-appeasement candidate against Quintin Hogg, who ran as a pro-Chamberlain Tory. Heath continued to develop his musical profile, singing in the renowned Bach Choir and performing Brahms *Requiem* in memory of King George V who died in 1935. On his visits to Europe Heath always found time to spend hours in art galleries. His contemporary, Denis Healey, was equally passionate about music and art but in the philistine Tory world Heath had to rise through, his deep culture was a private passion and rare in British politics which puts a premium on bluff, hearty Englishness and does not know how to deal with someone who loves and is deeply moved by European culture.

'I think he {Heath} was always very lonely. I would come home having made a great speech in the House and my wife would ask how many infinitives I had split. Or if I came home after a stinker of a day in the department she would give me a whiskey and calm me down. Poor Ted used to go back to that flat over Downing Street utterly alone with no-one to talk to.'

PETER WALKER

Heath left Oxford in 1939 a changed man. He spent the autumn on a curious debating tour of the United States – one of the more intriguing episodes of the 'Phoney War' when so much of life ran along normal lines. The annual trip by two of the best student debaters from British universities to debate with their opposite numbers in the United States is a much-prized opportunity to see America. Despite the outbreak of war it was decided to continue the visit. Like his travels in Europe, Heath got a chance to get to know America from top to bottom and understood that the United States, despite speaking English, is a profoundly foreign country with no more regard for British interests and needs than any other faraway land with its own different culture, politics and traditions.

The Heath of 1940 was already much formed. He had a girlfriend with whom he shared bike rides and concerts back in Kent but his passion was for music and his energies were reserved for politics. Did Heath ever have sex with a woman? The question is not important, yet the absence of women, of family, of the difficulties of sustaining a relationship with another person and one's children left Heath without some reference points that might have let him become a more rounded, a fuller human being as a political leader. His protégé and Cabinet colleague, Peter Walker, believes that Heath had one serious relationship in the past but once that broke down he just relapsed into permanent bachelor-hood. 'But he was marvelous with my five children and when he stayed at my house in Worcester for the Three Counties festival he would play cowboys and Indians with them and they adored him. I think he was always very lonely. I would come home having made a great speech in the House and my wife would ask how many infinitives I had split. Or if I came home after a stinker of a day in the department she would give me a whiskey and calm me down. Poor Ted used to go back to that flat over Downing Street utterly alone with no-one to talk to.'[6] Chris Patten, who was also selected by Heath to run the Conservative Research Department as a bright young Balliol graduate said it was 'difficult to like Ted. He just wasn't a likeable man'.[7] Patten's judgement was made in a tone of regret and sadness. A Labour generation of post-war politicians who had all been at Oxford in the 1930s became and stayed friends across many political divides. Heath in his autobiography claims in the last paragraph that *I have, and always have had, many friends in all walks of life*.[8] He protests too much. Heath was socially autistic. His self-centredness allowed him time to work and do things that those who have to bring up families lose in exchange for the unique joy of being a parent. Heath was never a fully-formed man. Oxford helped make him but he left Balliol still incomplete as a human being. But as with so many other young men unsure of their worth, their abilities and their role in life, Oxford opened many doors for Heath. Now he would go off to fight in a war and prepare for power.

Chapter 2: War and Into Parliament

Heath had a good war. He volunteered at the outbreak of war and enrolled in the Royal Artillery. He was posted as a Second Lieutenant to the 107th Heavy Anti-Aircraft Regiment which was defending Merseyside from *Luftwaffe* attacks. As at the Oxford Union, or his later service in the whips' office, it is his command of organisation that come to the fore. He became adjutant of his regiment with the rank of captain in March 1942. He also took charge of the battery band. Once he was traveling with the band to play in Chester in an ambulance an army medic had leant the musicians. It was caught up in a traffic jam and Heath used the stop to rehearse. A senior officer who turned up was astonished to hear dance music being played from the back of an ambulance. 'Typically', said a Colonel later, 'Heath had got his band rehearsing to avoid wasting time.'[1] Fellow officers noticed his obsession with paperwork. He was a stickler for detail, for doing things by the book. When his troops found an abandoned stock of champagne he would not drink it as it was, in his eyes, stolen property. One of his earlier commanding officers sent Heath to his next posting with the warning 'I am sending you the future Prime Minister of England.'[2] Before 1944 he travelled up and down the length of Britain mounting anti-aircraft defences. The army is one of Britain's great public institutions. Its order, hierarchy, tradition and history – and under pressure its ability to reinvent itself – makes the British Army in wartime an organisation in which hard work and politeness to superiors brings big rewards.

He arrived in France in July 1944 and was quickly in action before Caen. Later he suffered a scalp wound in December 1944 in the defence of Nijmegen. In 1945 he became battery commander with the rank of major and once the war was over he stayed in Germany until 1946 finishing with the rank of acting Lieutenant Colonel. Heath was mentioned in despatches in November 1944 and awarded a military MBE. At different parades and commemorations after the war he had as good an array of medals, some earned under fire, as any other senior politician and more than most. Heath made friends in the army, including Michael Fraser, who later rose to head the Conservative Party Central Office. Heath continued his military life as a reserve officer in the elite 'amateur' regiment, the Honourable Artillery Company (HAC). He took his duties seriously into the 1940s and the late 1950s. He was promoted to commanding officer of an HAC regiment and became Master Gunner at the Tower of London. He enjoyed the fortnight-long annual camp, turning up to act at as CO even if it meant dashing back to Westminster to vote. At a time when other men were well into marriage and watching children grow, Heath enjoyed the need for order, purpose and achievement that military hierarchy provides. In the post-war Tory ranks there were many medals on the coats of senior MPs at the time of Remembrance Sunday or other Second World War commemorations. Heath's decade as a military man, on active and reserve service, was an important part of his life. Unlike a later generation of Conservatives who ridiculed men like Helmut Kohl for whom Europe was, in his words, a question of 'war and peace', Heath knew a Europe of war and worked for a Europe of peace. The war had taken him to the heart of his beloved Europe. He looked askance at the destruction of the cities of Germany where he arrived with his regiment in 1945 to occupy Hanover. He told his brigade commander that his top priority was *to rebuild the opera house at Herrenhausen ... My men must have culture.*[3] But he was even more shocked to return in the early 1950s and see the cities rebuilt, the cafés full of young people, new economic and cultural energies being unleashed in peaceful directions and with more drive and modernisation than was evident in Britain. There is a journalist hidden in Heath, the need to be a witness and see great people and great events for himself. He returned to Nuremberg and saw the Nazi leaders on trial for their life. Churchill brought to life the vision of a 'kind of United States of Europe' in his famous speech in Zurich in September 1946. The wartime premier appealed for a reconciliation between France and Germany and outlined a prototype European Union. The speech caught a mood and offered a political path forward for a Europe still rocky and hesitantly rebuilding itself and still full of hatred and loathing from the previous decades of wars and occupations. Across the continent politicians and intellectuals of the democratic left and right seized Churchill's speech as their own manifesto to build a different politics.

The big exception was Labour in Britain. The Labour government and party refused to send any delegates to the founding congress of the European Movement in the Hague in 1948 which gave birth the Council of Europe, the European Convention of European Rights and the European Court of Human Rights. Attlee and Bevin were obsessed with the United States. They were obliged to concede a botched independence to Britain's imperial possessions in the sub-continent but left a divided Kashmir to fester and give rise to an Islamist fundamentalism. Bevin's policy in Palestine was a disaster as Britain left shiploads of Jewish asylum-seekers who had survived the Holocaust to sail around the Mediterranean under the glare of world publicity, unable to believe what British soldiers were doing to Jews. The Labour government remained deeply colonialist, shipping out men and women to Britain's African colonies, and still lived under the illusion that a economic zone dominated by sterling under British control or influence would be the best way forward for British interests.

Labour's refusal in 1950 to take part in the Schuman Plan which proposed putting Europe's steel and coal industries under a common supra-national authority with government, employer and union representatives on it further sidelined Britain from being a leader in post-war European politics.[4] For Heath, the willingness of Churchill and the Conservatives to offer leadership in Europe was further proof that his political choices made sense. He took a job as a civil servant in 1946, having come first in the administrative class examination, and went to work for the Ministry of Civil Aviation, although his recruiters wanted him to go and work in the Foreign Office. By 1947, however, he had already decided on a political career and needed a UK, and preferably London-based, job to pursue those ambitions.[5]

The average citizen of Great Britain still regards union in Europe as a distant ideal but not a practical proposition. On the continent, however, the man-in-the-street realizes the weakness of his nation in isolation.

HEATH

He was adopted as Conservative candidate for Bexley, a middle class part of south-east England where London suburbs blend into Kent towns. He had to resign from the Civil Service though his short period in Whitehall was helpful as a minister, he claimed. He found a job as news editor of the Anglo-Catholic weekly *Church Times*. In an unsigned editorial Heath made the case for Europe. *The average citizen of Great*

Britain still regards union in Europe as a distant ideal but not a practical proposition. On the continent, however, the man-in-the-street realizes the weakness of his nation in isolation. But it was politics, not journalism, that remained his burning purpose in life. His new constituency was close to home. Heath stayed with his parents. His brother had followed Teddy neither to Oxford nor to an army commission and a professional career. Teddy was alone with a father who was now his own boss of a small business – rather like Margaret Thatcher's upbringing in the home of a struggling small businessman where every penny was hard-earned and the world of taxation, fair treatment of workers, and the widespread extension of the state's role and authority after 1945 was resented. Margaret Roberts, as she then was, was also a candidate for the Kent seat of Dartford which Labour managed to hold in the elections of 1950 and 1951, thus depriving the young Oxford graduate the chance of entering the House of Commons at the same time as the man whom she replaced as Leader of the Conservative Party.

Heath and Thatcher were entwined from the late 1940s onwards and defined British Conservatism for more than half a century. Heath set about winning his seat held by the clever Labour intellectual and educationalist, Ashley Bramall, with the same dedicated organisation that he showed at Oxford and in the Army. Six decades later, as party activism dwindles and party politics is mediated via an elite media and London-based policy elites paid by influence-seeking corporate groups and wealthy individuals, it is hard to recreate the political involvement of millions in the 1940s. My history teacher at school in the 1960s told us how he subscribed to Hansard in order to read each night the debates in the Commons and the details of the decisions taken that would reshape Britain. Political participation in parties reached an all-time high in this period – the Young Conservatives alone grew to more than one million members. Heath personally knocked on the doors along with his party team of 25,000 households in his constituency as he sought to win it. He clearly was popular. Heath was not quite bright enough to be recruited to work for Conservative Central Office alongside intellectuals like Enoch Powell and Iain Macleod. After the owners of the *Church Times* became nervous at having a political activist and Tory candidate as their news editor, he moved to work as a trainee banker in October 1949 with the long-established City merchant bank, Brown Shipley. Close to the Conservative Party, the bank allowed Heath all the time he needed to nurse his seat. He supported the modernisation of the Conservative Party set in hand by R A Butler which endorsed the welfare state changes that the Labour government introduced after 1945. In particular, the Conservatives would not revert to the anti-union ideology in force under Baldwin and Chamberlain in the 1920s and 1930s. Butler accepted that a future Conservative government would protect basic employment rights for workers and work constructively with trade unions.

Heath spoke at party conferences and weekend seminars, joined Tory dining clubs, and worked hard at winning his seat. Heath later wrote: *I joined most of the sporting, cultural, business and purely social organisations, attending just about every function held there between 1947 and 1950. I made more speeches, presented more prizes and danced more waltzes than I had ever done in my life.*[6] He sent an election address to every household, promising support for full employment policies, further developments in social policy, tax cuts and *closer association with Western Europe and America which Mr Churchill has done so much to foster.* The victory was desperately close. After two recounts, Heath had a majority of just 133. The Communist candidate had polled 481 votes. Conservative candidates had done well in Kent seats, save in Dartford where the future Mrs Thatcher failed to be elected.

Chapter 3: Rising Front-Bencher

Heath made his mark almost immediately in the Commons. He was a former President of the Oxford Union, a Lieutenant Colonel in the most prestigious Territorial Army regiment, a man with a good war record. He sat in the Smoking Room, the most club-like of the many places in Westminster where drink is available. A non-smoker himself, he put up with clouds of tobacco smoke because it was in the Smoking Room that the greats of the Commons, from Churchill to Aneurin Bevan, would come to be convivial and be admired. Heath made an important speech – his maiden speech – in support of Europe but more significant was helping to set up the One Nation group of Conservative MPs, which included future cabinet members and dominant figures in the party after 1950 like Reginald Maudling, Iain Macleod, Enoch Powell, Angus Maude and Robert Carr – a powerful network of new MPs who arrived in 1950 and who dominated Tory politics during the Heath era. Each member of the group wrote a chapter in a book which set out policy of housing, social services, education, health, pensions, and the disabled. Heath's chapter was on the financing of social services. The One Nation doctrine accepted that 'full employment is a first responsibility of government', a belief Heath never deviated from. Twice a week, the group met, working on their ideas and papers, writing and re-writing them under the pressure of mutual criticism and support. Decades later such work was derided as policy wonking. Yet all successful political parties, in and out of office, have to keep producing their own analysis of the problems of the moment and how to craft solutions that get voters and party activists to say, as it were, 'Yes – that's the way forward'. One Nation was in tune with the leadership of the Conservative Party. The backbench Labour MP and intellectual, Richard Crossman, noted in his diary 'the general make-up of the Churchill Cabinet means that it will be only very slightly to the right of the most recent Attlee Cabinet'.[1] Heath was going to stay firmly in the middle-ground of Conservative ideology. It was the way to move up, and it was where he felt at home.

One of the One Nation MPs, John Rodgers, said 'Heath was no intellectual. He listened while intellectuals like Macleod, Maude or Powell pontificated. Then he would surface with something like "Well, what are we going to do about it?"'[2] Heath appreciated the value and force of ideas in politics. During his ascent to leadership he made sure he was at the heart of policy-making. He persuaded Macmillan to set up what was called the Steering Committee which the Conservative Party historians John Barnes and Richard Cockett describe as 'an extremely powerful institution, in effect an inner cabinet focusing on policy for the next election – although some of the ideas generated were sufficiently attractive to warrant the government's immediate attention'.[3] After the 1964 election defeat, Heath chaired the key Conservative Party policy body, the Advisory Committee on Policy and when he became Prime Minister, of course, Heath set up the Central Policy Review Staff unit as his own think-tank within 10 Downing Street. Heath knew full well that in politics success goes to those who control the commanding heights of policy ideas. But for Heath ideas were subordinate to action. He sailed on the surface of politics. The deeper intellectual and value currents which shape and over time alter the navigation charts of successful politics, often more quickly than is realised, were not Heath's forte.

This brief foray into policy-making and the catchy concept of One Nation Toryism helped Heath to be at the centre of the new Conservative Party that was coming into being in response to the defeat of 1945 and the new social contract forged by Labour, including the creation of the National Health Service, the extension of redistributive welfare provision with increased payments for mothers, pensioners, and scholarships to allow working class children who went to grammar school to go to Oxford and Cambridge and other universities without the financial worries that had almost prevented Heath from enjoying a university education. These moves were part of a general Western move to a fairer society and a greater role for collective and state action to ensure that the conditions which gave rise to fascism in pre-war Europe were not replicated. To combat Communism and mobilise populations against the threat of what was seen as expansive Sovietism, a new alliance between parties of the right and trade unions was necessary. In West Europe, most governments had gone further than Labour in nationalising key sectors of the economy. In Nordic countries, trade unions ruthlessly expelled Communist and other leftist militants so that Nordic social democracy, with its alliance between global business and welfarist trade unions, was able to develop. In Germany, Ludwig Erhard, the economic genius who created the German economic miracle in the long years of Chancellor Adenaur's reign, invented the *Sozialmarkwirtschaft*, which sought to allow space for market-driven capitalism but in conjunction with social justice.

Labour might have been able to capitalise on the growing prosperity of the 1950s in most western democracies – the

'You've never had it so good' years to use Macmillan's formulation. Attlee had a working, if small, majority of five after the 1950 election, but Labour had run out of steam. Too many key ministers had been in office for a decade. They were unable to come up with new ideas. Renewing a government while still in office is the trickiest of political arts, and Attlee had no idea how to do it. Faced with the resignation of Aneurin Bevan and Harold Wilson over attempts to finance health services by obliging people to accept some responsibility themselves for its growing costs, the Labour Prime Minister simply gave in and called a general election in October 1951.

Labour won more votes than the Conservatives which in most countries would mean a Labour prime minister in Downing Street. But the vagaries of the British electoral system, based on individual constituencies of different sizes, meant that the Conservatives were back in power with a majority of sixteen. Heath's own majority went up to 1,629. He fought the election against a background of his mother battling cancer and dying ten days before the 1951 election. Each evening Heath played to his fading mother the pieces she loved on the piano she had watched her beloved Teddy master as a boy. *It was a devastating blow for me, the first I had sustained in my family life and one that I hardly knew how to handle,*[4] wrote Heath. He had been a mother's boy. She had pushed him at school and to aim for Oxford. He stayed with his parents regularly as a candidate and young MP. Now Heath would be on his own emotionally, unable to or indifferent to finding a woman to share his life or replace the mother who had always been there. His father lived on until 1976, dying aged 88. He married twice after the death of Teddy's mother and Heath never took to his new stepmothers. Henceforth there was an emptiness in his life.

Anyone who is an MP knows the tremendous solace in times of personal distress or unhappiness that the Commons can be. It provides a home from home, company at all times of day and evening, endlessly interesting work and often high drama as the affairs that grip the nation unfold in the intimacies of the Chamber, the Lobbies, the corridors and one of the most comfortable, spacious, silent reader and work friendly libraries in the world. In addition, to be a government minister when personal tragedy befalls is to have a constant flow of work and decisions that fill the time that otherwise might be left for introspection and self-pity. Heath was lucky to go straight from mourning his mother's death to the front bench as soon as Churchill formed his new government.

Heath had already been appointed an unpaid whip in January 1951. He caviled at taking the job. It would mean no chance to speak in the Commons either on One Nation issues or to raise in the Chamber constituency cases in what was still an ultra-marginal seat. But the Tory grandee and former party chairman, Lord Swinton, gave him clear advice: 'You should take it, my boy. You cannot tell where it will lead but it is the first step on the ladder. The rest

Another Conservative prime minister, John Major, spent the first part of his ministerial career rising through the ranks of the whips' office and rhapsodised about it, giving the institution a capital 'O' in his memoirs. 'It exists to deliver the government's business and will do so even if the collective view of the Office is that the legislation is unwise. Ministers, even prime ministers, might be shocked by the robust opinions expressed about their policies, performance or personalities by the whips. The Office is nobody's patsy, as politicians with an arrogant streak have often learned. This is invaluable, because the whips know the collective view of the parliamentary party better by far than any minister, and are able to make that view known as policy is brought forward.'[5]

is up to you.'[6] Heath stepped onto the parliamentary career escalator and did not leave until thrown off 25 years later.

For the adjutant Heath, the meticulous record-keeper who had been scorer for his school's First Eleven, the whips' office was the most perfect place to build his reputation for efficiency and well-organised command and control politics. His military rank and continuing service as a Lieutenant Colonel with the Honourable Artillery Company gained him entry into the coterie of whips. Prime Ministers get two types of whips' offices – those they want or those they need. Heath worked steadily in the 1950s to make sure the whips' office was one that a Conservative prime minister needed. He was made a full whip, adding £500 as a junior minister to his MP's salary of £1,000. Heath was always on duty, staying late at night to make certain that Tory MPs were present in numbers to get through legislation. Being a whip is an essential part of all democratic governments. They have different names in different legislatures around the world but the task is the same – to persuade, corral, menace a group of vain, ambitious, self-centred individuals that they must surrender part of their individual belief and conscience and vote for legislation which the government believes is necessary for the good administration of the country and will help win the next election. Whips need to know each MP's weakness, to handle individual MPs as they face problems over policy, or difficulties in their constituency, with their private lives or personal finances.

Heath simply worked harder and longer than his fellow whips. In the 730 parliamentary divisions between his entering the Commons in 1950 and 1955, Heath voted in 720 and was paired in six.[7] Few MPs then or now spent or spend as much time physically present in Westminster. He was entrusted with difficult messages to Winston Churchill, telling the ageing leader he had to turn up to vote himself or stay into the small hours to face down Labour efforts to delay or derail legislation by all the means that parliamentary manoeuvring allows.[8] The officers' mess style of the Tory whips' office presented no problems to Lt-Col Heath but he did not join in their clubby get-togethers and rarely bought his round. Instead he maintained his interest in policy and spoke at weekends to as many Conservative seminars or study groups as possible. He impressed the Young Conservatives at their summer conference with his ability to speak for an hour without notes, and with his fluency and clarity. The wooden Heath that television viewers saw when Prime Minister was quite different from the impressive, confident speaker who, as the author can testify, was able to hold the Commons or a large dinner gathering in his hand so fluent was his way with arguments, facts, or a telling image that combines to make a natural public speaker.

In the Commons and the country, Heath was not to be heard. He made himself popular with fellow MPs by supporting a 75 per cent increase in an MP's salary. He was well-regarded by Churchill who dined with him at the Whips' table in the Members' Dining Room and was one of the few to be informed when the ageing Prime Minister suffered a stroke. He started the practice of keeping records on all MPs so that he built up a reputation for all-knowing competence. And since he had no wife, partner, children or family home to go to in London he was always to be found at the Commons in the morning before business started and in the Conservative clubs just above the Mall in which gossip is exchanged and policies are nudged this way and that. Heath had to straddle, on one hand, the old-style county and ex-military MPs or sons of peers for whom being an MP was a duty and who were content to be backbenchers and, on the other hand, the new ambitious public and grammar school, full-time professional

MPs whose ambition for office was overweening. Helped by a Labour Party which was bitterly split along left-right lines and where an ageing group of leaders who refused to make way for younger talent held sway, Heath managed to make the Conservative Party in Parliament look competent and deserving of re-election in 1955 under their new leader Sir Anthony Eden.

Eden rewarded the able young whip with promotion to the Chief Whip's post at the age of 39. A Chief Whip attends Cabinet meetings though he is not a full member of the Cabinet. Heath was now at the epicentre of political power and authority in Britain. Immediately he was plunged into a crisis – Suez – that would have tested any Chief Whip, but it was the making of Ted Heath. He had already shown a sure hand in a Conservative Party which was losing the deference to a Prime Minister that Churchill had enjoyed. What today would be called 'rebels' started to form into loose blocs around issues like calling for a more robust right-wing economic and social policy and a reduction of the state sector in the economy. On international policy there was a resurgence of latter-day imperialism with Tory MPs unhappy about the pace of pulling down the Union Jack from colonies or urging more aggressive military action against national independence movements. Even on Europe, where Heath's sympathies lay with pro-Europeans, he had to fall in behind Eden's hostility to Britain taking any effective part in the negotiations culminating in the Treaty of Rome. Heath actively and successfully discouraged pro-European Tory MPs like Geoffrey Rippon and Fred Corfield who in July 1956 organised a motion attracting the signature of 84 Conservative and three Liberal MPs which called for the creation of a common market in western Europe with Britain as a member.[9]

Suez saw the two main parties opposing each other on the

most important issue that MPs ever have to vote on – whether to endorse the sending of young citizens to risk their lives to defend Britain's national interest as defined by the government of the day. Normally on issues of war and peace there is a broad national consensus. In the South African conflict at the beginning of the 20th century or the Iraq conflict a century later, that national consensus was quickly shown to be lacking. Suez was a greater challenge as the Labour leadership, after some uncertainty, moved fully into outright opposition to the use of armed force against Nasser's decision to take over control of the Suez Canal.

Heath worked around the clock to stop the Conservative Party in Parliament from wrecking itself in mutual destructive anger. He mixed charm and cajolement with threats to call constituency officers if MPs voted against the government. As the scale of Eden's humiliation by the United States became apparent, the anger of right-wing Tories increased. Their fury boiled over at the news of Britain's withdrawal. But again Heath found ways to persuade angry Conservative MPs not to help Labour's no confidence motion. Eden was destroyed but Heath kept the Conservative Party intact ready to be handed over, despite the months of Suez trauma, to a new leader, Harold Macmillan.

'He is a very likeable man. He is not a snob. He is natural except for a rather embarrassing habit of shaking his shoulders up and down when he laughs – and he laughs a great deal.'

THE OBSERVER ON HEATH

Like Heath, Macmillan was a Balliol and Oxford Union man, strongly pro-European. Heath knew Eden was doomed and the whips' office quietly canvassed Conservative MPs over the Christmas recess. He reported that few wanted Butler to become Prime Minister and this together with the majority view of the Cabinet and most party grandees in the shires and constituencies led to

Harold Macmillan going to the Palace. Heath was sent to tell Butler in person that he would not be Prime Minister. Macmillan dined with Heath at the Turf Club off Piccadilly on the evening of his appointment as Prime Minister. The new Prime Minister took Heath's advice on bringing into the government both pro-Suez right-wingers like Julian Amery, who was also a strong pro-European and to bring back the liberal Sir Edward Boyle who had resigned as a minister in protest at Suez. He urged Macmillan to stand firm against the efforts of his Chancellor, Peter Thorneycroft, who wanted to impose major cuts in public expenditure as part of an ideological bid to turn the Conservatives back to their pre-war economic thinking. Heath was more than a parliamentary manager for Macmillan. He was ever-present with advice on how to appear on television. He encouraged the promotion of his generation of liberal Conservatives like Reginald Maudling who had been at Merton College when Heath was at Balliol but who openly asked his contemporaries which was the best party to join to get on in politics.[10] There was no Heath faction as such. Heath had quietly cultivated political editors and they responded by praising his handling of the Suez crisis and writing him up as a coming man. 'He is a very likeable man. He is not a snob. He is natural except for a rather embarrassing habit of shaking his shoulders up and down when he laughs – and he laughs a great deal,' noted the *Observer* in 1959.[11] Everyone likes someone who laughs and finds something to laugh about. In the 1959 election, Macmillan came to Heath's seat and said he represented 'everything that is best in the new progressive modern Tory Party … He stands for the new philosophy and modern thought in the party.'[12] The Conservatives won their third election in a row. Edward Heath got his reward. Not yet a decade in the Commons, he entered the Cabinet.

Chapter 4: Into Cabinet

In the Churchill Museum, next to the War Cabinet complex underneath the Treasury in Whitehall, a copy of the Atlantic Charter signed by Roosevelt and Churchill is on display. Article 5 commits the Allies to 'the object of securing for all improved labour standards'. In the 21st century, trade unions are not given much prominence in the affairs of state, but in the 1950s, good government in Britain, the rest of Europe, the United States, Canada, Australia and even Japan required a social contract with organised labour that placed trade unions as key intermediaries in labour market management. All these democracies had passed laws protecting trade unions as part of the post-1945 compact between employers, governments and unions, and some had gone further by formally giving unions exclusive rights to negotiate and sign wage contracts. British unions wanted the protection of the law for some of their activities. The 1945 Labour government had repealed legislation enacted after the 1926 failed General Strike. Giving unions new legal immunities did Attlee little good politically as some unions sought to use their influence in the Labour Party to impose pro-Soviet, protectionist, or syndicalist policies upon the elected government. Attlee saw off such challenges but it was a lesson that just because unions were an integral part of the Labour Party this did not mean they would support a Labour government against their own sectional interests or sectarian ideology.[1] Uniquely in Europe, British trade union practice was based where possible on the closed shop. This required workers to be union members to get or keep jobs. No union wanted to be told by law what to do or not do. So Britain had no minimum wage, nor legal recognition rights for unions. Within the union movement itself there was a continuous struggle for influence and control between Communists and their opponents. Not all pro-communists carried a party card but the influence of trade unions in the Labour Party meant that the best way for Communists, and by the end of the 1960s, for the Trotskyists and other leftists, to transform ideology in to practice was to climb the trade union ladder.

Britain's greatest trade union leader of the 20th century, Ernest Bevin, had helped win support for a place for organised labour as an estate of the realm after 1945 by his doughty patriotism in the war and his ruthless organisation of British factories, mines and the working class to deliver the weapons to win the war. Later he committed the Labour Party and the British government to a global conflict with Communism. In the 1950s, public opinion polls consistently showed support for the trade unions. In 1958, when Heath was Labour minister, 61 per cent of the public thought unions were a 'good thing' for Britain and 15 per cent did not.[2] There had been a growth in unofficial strikes and shop steward power. Unlike the United States, Germany or Nordic countries where unions had their own rules requiring strike action to be approved by two-thirds or even 75 per cent of all members, shop stewards in Britain on the basis of a casually organised mass meeting and a show of hands could shut down a workplace. The film *'I'm all right Jack'* captured the atmosphere. Slowly the questions of trade union authority, power and impact of productivity and economic performance was moving up the political agenda. In due course, the issue would become central to Heath's tenure as Prime Minister, culminating in the 1974 election which he called and lost over the issue of trade union power within Britain.

Churchill had sought to continue the politics of co-operation with the unions. His labour minister, Walter Monckton, was told to soothe rather than wrestle with the unions. A big bus strike in London in 1958, under a new left-wing leadership in the Transport and General Workers' Union, showed how effective union militant action could be in disrupting public services and the lives of ordinary citizens. In the 1950s, the Conservatives needed to win workers' votes. To launch a frontal attack on workers' organisations made little electoral sense. But an increasingly inefficient labour market system in Britain raised the question of reform. Full employment and a labour market under the influence of the closed shop led to wage increases unjustified by productivity improvements or the profits of companies. Unlike the social democratic unions in northern Europe which accepted a broad responsibility to promote productivity improvements and collaborated with employers to achieve this, the level of such codetermination in Britain was limited by unions competing with each other as much as with the bosses. British unions steadfastly refused to learn from best practice in other countries in this period and periodic attempts by TUC reformers, like the insightful General Secretary George Woodcock, were seen off by individual union leaders who were not willing to share any of their sovereign control over the unions for the greater good of all employees.

Heath thus became Minister for Labour in the autumn of 1959 at a turning point in the government's approach to industrial relations and labour market reform. According to Andrew Taylor, the historian of the Conservative Party's approach to trade unions, Macmillan's approach was based on the view that 'any intervention had to take place within the established framework of union-government co-operation. The government's view was that industrial unrest and wage inflation were the product of ignorance, and could be remedied by management taking employees into their confidence and by government publicising the economic facts of life to encourage wage moderation'.[3] Others like Iain Macleod and Enoch Powell were urging either legal reforms or pushing to allow the market and money supply to stop agreeing inflationary wage deals, especially in the nationalised and public sectors where, by definition, any wages not covered by the income generated by the industry or service were a form of subsidy from other tax-payers.

All this swirled around Heath as the new Minister for Labour. But he focused on solving problems rather than developing a deeper political response or forging a new philosophy to handle the trade union question. When he rose to answer departmental questions in November 1959, the first time he had spoken in the Commons for nine years, above all he wanted to show his command of the Despatch Box. Competence at the Despatch Box remains the *sine qua non* for an effective ministerial career. The Commons is kind to its own, but when an MP leaves the backbenches for the Treasury Bench, he or she is judged by different, harder standards. 'There but for the grace of a lack of patron or a prime minister who knows I exist, might go I', is what most government backbenchers think as they see contemporaries, rivals or, worst of all, much younger colleagues promoted. Heath demanded

> *The atmosphere of co-operation, coupled with the high level of social services, confirmed my belief that good industrial relations were both the product of, and essential to, a prosperous and fair society.*
>
> HEATH

endless briefings from his officials for the questions he had to answer and to their surprise read all his papers thoroughly. In his speeches in the Commons and in reply to questions, he was much better at speaking spontaneously rather than at delivering prepared scripts.

His relations with union leaders were correct – polite but stiff. He came over to them more as a civil servant than a political minister. He invited union leaders to private meals and was surprised when the right-wing leader of the Amalgamated Engineering Union, Bill Carron, accepted but on the condition that the meal take place at the Tory Carlton Club where no-one would recognise the union chief eating with the Tory minister.[4] The lunch, well-oiled, lasted until 4 p.m. Heath contrasts this reluctance on the part of British union leaders to take the proffered hand of friendship with what he saw in Sweden a few months later where he *was struck by how much the two sides socialised together. The atmosphere of cooperation, coupled with the high level of social services, confirmed my belief that good industrial relations were both the product of, and essential to, a prosperous and fair society.*[5] Like other admirers of Swedish labour market arrangements then and since, Heath admired the end but refused to consider the means to achieve that end. In Sweden, this included a hegemonic social democratic led government which had been in power since the 1930s. Swedish trade unions were based on one single union covering all workers in each of the main industries. The Swedish equivalent of the TUC negotiated wages for all workers from the centre – a concept utterly at odds with the British tradition of individual company by company bargaining and multi-unionism.

Instead of rising to the challenge of creating a new philosophy of labour market organisation which might move British unions and employers in a new direction, Heath contented himself with staying in the furrow ploughed by Churchill and Macmillan. He passed his first test by helping prevent a national railway strike at the beginning of 1960 by bringing the leaders of the three unions and the managers of the state-run rail industry to his office. He offered them 5 per cent as an interim rise, which they gladly accepted as it meant a significant increase in real wages. Heath was under pressure from Conservative MPs who wanted to begin a process of trade union reform. He rejected their suggestion of setting up a Royal Commission on Trade Unions aimed at creating a new legislative framework for unions. They noted his 'policy of avoiding any annoyance to the trade unions'. Heath did submit a Cabinet memorandum suggesting that the Prime Minister chair a conference to discuss a new approach to industrial relations. His suggestion was turned down in the full Cabinet which wanted some guarantee that both employers and unions would accept a linkage between pay, profits and productivity. Heath's proposed conference would simply be a talking shop.

Heath was Minister for Labour for little more than a year so it is unfair to ask why he failed to solve the labour market and industrial relations problems that helped bring down succeeding governments including his own. His instincts were generous. Neither the market nor law, on their own, will deliver social justice and rising prosperity for the broad mass of a working population. Unions are an essential intermediary. But Britain's unions could not rise to the challenge of reforming themselves. Heath had no real thought-through philosophy of reform. He was suspicious of the analysis of right-wingers like Enoch Powell. Logic might be on their side but the implementation of such policy would produce opposition from unions that would do damage to any sense of a fair society.

When appointed Minister for Labour in 1959 Heath had asked Macmillan to be kept in the post for the full five years of a parliament in order to master the job much as he had mastered the business of being an effective whip and Chief Whip. Events decided things differently. Heath was soon to be plunged into the politics that would make his name – Europe.

Chapter 5: Into Europe and Party Leadership

Heath was Prime Minister for only 44 months – three years and 259 days to be precise. In that period he took one of the most momentous decisions of any 20th-century prime minister – to take Britain into Europe. The anger and splits in his own and other parties that arose still reverberate. Like the prime minister who invented the Conservative Party, Robert Peel, whose free trade reform in the 1840s changed the country, Heath fundamentally altered the direction and destiny of Britain by going into Europe. He did so against much conventional wisdom and the wishes of the Whitehall establishment which always is suspicious of foreign entanglements save doing most of what Washington wants. No Prime Minister since then has been willing to show equivalent leadership on Europe. And unlike his forerunners in Downing Street, once the European question was on the agenda, Heath did not duck away from the implications of shared sovereignty or the political implications of entering into a treaty relationship with other European nations. Heath was willing to link Britain's defence and military profile with that of France, including sharing nuclear weapons. In 2006, the historian David Starkey, a self-proclaimed Conservative, described Heath as Britain's worst prime minister, as bad 'as Lord North'. Starkey's contempt is still shared by many Conservative politicians and their puffers in the media. Heath's other difficulties as Prime Minister in the early 1970s – inflation, economic management, union law problems – have faded with time. But a large part of the British establishment still have not come to terms with Britain being fully part of the European Union.

The signs were clear from the moment Heath rose to make his maiden speech in the Commons. Churchill had set the tone on Europe for post-1945 British politics with his appeal in Zurich in 1946 'to re-create the European family, or as much of it as we can, and provide it with a structure under which it can dwell in peace, in safety and in freedom. We must build a kind of United States of Europe'. Churchill's speech spurred the movement for European unity much as his Fulton 'Iron Curtain' speech helped create Atlanticist anti-Soviet politics. The European movement was launched at a giant conference in the Hague, followed by the creation of the Council of Europe, based in Strasbourg. Conservatives led by Harold Macmillan and Duncan Sandys took an enthusiastic part in these European gatherings. Ernest Bevin told the TUC annual conference in September 1947 that there was a need for a customs union between Britain, Western Europe and the Commonwealth.[1] Bevin, in common with other Labour ministers, was willing to explore joining with European countries in some relationship in order to promote British interests and place in the post-war world. What none of the Labour cabinet could contemplate was a sharing of national sovereign power and a willingness to have some supra-national authority deciding policy.

In private, Attlee, Bevin and Dalton made unpleasant xenophobic remarks about continental Europeans. This sturdy John Bullism always plays well with a British establishment and a populist press that is superior about Paris, snobbish about Bonn, and supine about Washington. But it left pro-European politics in Britain between 1945 and 1990 dominated by Conservative rather than Labour politicians. Heath first went to Paris in 1931 as a 14-year old and said he fell in love with the French capital. He was a relentless visitor to different European countries as schoolboy, undergraduate, soldier, and candidate. Thus it made sense to use the two-day debate in the Commons in June 1950, exactly a decade after Churchill had proposed to fuse British and French citizenship to forge unity against fascism, to urge British co-operation with the efforts to find European unity.

Labour's Chancellor of the Exchequer, Stafford Cripps, laughed at Heath in the Commons when the new MP suggested Britain should take part in the discussions aimed at creating a supranational High Authority for Europe's steel and coal industries. Heath replied: *The Chancellor of the Exchequer spoke looking at the worst point of view the whole time. He spoke of the high authority, suggesting that we should have no say in arranging the power of the high authority. Surely that would not be the case. He said we should be taking a risk with the whole of the economy. We on this side of the House felt that, by standing aside from the discussions, we may be taking a very great risk with our economy in coming years — a very great risk indeed. He said it would be also a great risk if we went in and then withdrew. We regard it as a greater risk to stand aside altogether at this stage.*[2]

The Chancellor of the Exchequer spoke looking at the worst point of view the whole time.... He said it would be also a great risk if we went in and then withdrew. We regard it as a greater risk to stand aside altogether at this stage.

HEATH

For Schuman and Monnet, of course, their aim was to bind in Germany in such a way that the divisions which had led to three German invasions and occupations of France in the previous 80 years could never happen again. Britain, uninvaded, unoccupied, unfazed by the obsessions of Paris and the Benelux nations (Belgium, Netherlands, Luxembourg) to change forever the way European nations, and especially Germany related to each other, was unable to see Europe as continental Europeans saw it. As Attlee told a reporter in the 1960s, 'I'm not very keen on the Common Market. After all, we beat Germany, and we beat Italy and we saved France, Belgium and Holland. I never see why we should go crawling to them.' His wartime boss, Churchill, did not share this mentality. Speaking in the debate in June 1950, Churchill told the Labour front bench: 'We are prepared to consider and, if convinced, to accept the abrogation of national sovereignty, provided we are satisfied with the conditions and safeguards ... national sovereignty is not inviolable, and it may be safely diminished for the sake of all the men in all the countries finding their way home together.'[3] Heath had kept in touch with German opinion. His Balliol friend, the Rhodes Scholar Philip Kaiser, was now a US representative at the International Labour Organisation in Geneva where Europe's unions, employers and governments met. Kaiser visited Heath in 1950 and kept him in touch with the growing continental support, backed as much by the social democratic left as by the new Christian democratic political groupings, for more European integration. And unlike the wishful thinking in London, what was desired was not simply greater economic cooperation. Heath had been in Bonn that summer. He was the first British MP to attend a dinner at the recently re-opened German embassy in Belgrave Square. Unlike Ernest Bevin, who said of the Germans 'I can't 'elp it, but I 'ates them', Germany was the source of Heath's beloved music – Bach, Schubert, Brahms. At a dinner in his honour at the German Embassy in London in 1998 he rhapsodised about German wines. Unlike so many in Britain, of all parties, Heath liked Germany and Germans. Hitlerism was an aberration. The Germany of Goethe, Beethoven and the great scientists, engineers, and democratic politicians that Heath met from the 1940s onwards was the Germany he believed in and wished well. He told the Commons that in his judgement the Germans' *attitude was governed entirely by political considerations. I believe there is a genuine desire on their part to reach agreement with France and with the other countries of Western Europe. I believe that in that desire the German government are genuine and I believe, too, that the German government would be prepared to make economic sacrifices in order to achieve those political results which they desire.* Britain taking part in the Schuman Plan discussions, *would give us a chance of leading Germany into the way we want her to go.*[4]

Heath's appeal fell on deaf ears. Britain would talk the talk on Europe but refused to walk the walk with other big European nations. Heath went into the Whips Office partly as a result of this speech, which was praised by Eden and Churchill. In the 1950s, Britain tried to shape a European defence profile by setting up the Western European Union (WEU) – a loose gathering of nations, both in and out of Nato, which agreed common defence goals. The WEU had a parliamentary assembly in which American and Canadian parliamentarians sat but has never had control over the military decisions of WEU members. But as with the Council of Europe, London would never concede any effective supranational power in partnership with other European nations. Churchill, Eden and Macmillan, who had been so keen on Europe up to 1951, found reasons in office to keep European integration at arm's length. The British sought to create a loose free trade association, which eventually took form as the European Free Trade Association. It left all decisions in the hands of national governments whose ability to resist economic patriotism or the special pleadings of lobbies for protectionist quotas or tariffs was limited.

In 1955 and 1956, politicians and officials in Paris, Bonn, Rome and the Benelux capitals began serious talks on creating a Common Market. Despite appeals from pro-British politicians on the continent for ministerial engagement in these discussions, Britain sent a minor Board of Trade official. Neither Eden nor Macmillan when he became Prime Minister in 1957 were willing to take the plunge into shaping the new Europe. That was left to politicians in France, Germany, Italy, Belgium, and the Netherlands. The Dutch, in particular, as a protestant, oceanic, liberal, free-trade nation were disappointed at the indifference shown by London. Monnet was hated by de Gaulle and he made every effort to persuade Britain to join the Common Market precisely so that French dominance would be matched by Britain. Heath took Monnet to speak at Oxford, frightening the elderly Frenchman as he drove at high speed along the A40. As Chief Whip, Heath was privy to the Cabinet rejection of British participation in the creation of the European Community. But his job was to defend and implement the Prime Minister's decisions, not challenge them.

By 1960, it was clear that the Common Market was here to stay and would flourish. Officials told ministers of their concern that a free market for industrial goods which excluded Britain would be bad for British industry which would not face the competitive challenge to upgrade continuing poor productivity. Washington began hinting that the United States saw the EEC six as their future partner, not exclusively Britain. The Cabinet was warned by the Chancellor, Derek Heathcoat-Amory, that joining the EEC 'would be a political act with economic consequences, not vice-versa'.[5]

Harold Macmillan accepted the point, telling the Commons in July 1961 when he announced Britain's bid for EEC membership, 'This is a political as well as an economic issue. Although the Treaty of Rome is concerned with economic matters it has an important political objective, namely to promote unity and stability in Europe.'[6] Writing in 1962 Macmillan confronted those who argued that the EEC was simply a kind of free trade area and Britain should participate only on economic grounds. 'It is true, of course, that political unity is the central aim of these European countries and we would naturally accept that goal ... As a member of the Community, Britain would have a strong voice in deciding the nature and timing of political unity. By remaining outside, we could be faced with a political solution in Europe which went counter to our interests, but which we could do nothing to influence.'

In the government reshuffle just before the summer recess of 1960, Macmillan decided to make the Earl of Home Foreign Secretary. Old Etonian commoner Macmillan undoubtedly felt happy with old Etonian aristocrat Home at the Foreign Office. However the symbolism of the Conservatives at the beginning of the societal, generational and cultural revolutions that made the 1960s the most exciting decade in 20th-century Britain searching amongst hereditary aristocrats to find a senior Cabinet minister seemed archaic. To be sure, Prime Ministers do not want independent Foreign Secretaries and having one in the Lords sent out a signal that Macmillan and Macmillan alone would decide Britain's foreign policy. The Foreign Office needed a minister in the Commons. With Macmillan's thoughts now turning to Europe he chose his loyal adjutant, Ted Heath, described by the *Sunday Times* 'as Mr Macmillan's favourite political son'[7] to explain foreign policy to MPs and British policy to Europeans.

Although the formal decision to apply for EEC member-ship was not announced until July 1961, Heath spent the months before touring every corner of Europe to assess the chances of a bid being successful and explaining Britain's and his desire to get closer to Europe. Heath received support from the newly-elected Kennedy administration. The US Under-Secretary of State, George Ball, met Heath in March 1961 and told him that America regarded the moves towards European unity 'as a major contribution to Western solidar-ity and the stability of the free world ... if Great Britain now decides to participate in the formidable efforts to unite Europe, she can, and I am sure she will, apply her unique political genius ... toward the creation of a unity that can transform the Western world.' In a private meeting with de Gaulle in June 1961 Kennedy urged the French president to support British entry. De Gaulle doubted Britain's will-ingness to accept the full conditions of EEC membership including dissolving the Commonwealth preference system. The French president's forebodings were kept private but they were prescient.

Heath went into the negotiations as if he was planning D-Day. He got the best and brightest of top Whitehall mandarins into a negotiating team. Each had to be fluent in three languages. Heath would meet with fellow foreign ministers in conclave while officials tested words and sought agreement to deal with New Zealand lamb meat, Austral-ian wool, or Canadian wheat. Jobsworths in Whitehall made his life as difficult as possible. A Community regulation laid down that fruit and vegetables should not be stacked with the choicest products on the top for the shopper to admire while the shopkeeper served onto the scale inferior-quality tomatoes or pears from behind. The Ministry of Agriculture gravely informed Heath it would take 15 years of a transition period to train the inspectors – the number needed was judged to be 52 – to go around Britain's greengrocers making them conform to European rules. Heath had to put forward this position as the settled UK government line. Sicco Mansholt, the Commission vice-president, responded: 'While listening to Mr Heath explain his government's present policy, I could not help wondering whether in 1940, at the blackest moments of the war Mr Churchill would have demanded fifteen years in which to train fifty-two pear and tomato inspectors to achieve the victory of which he was the creator.' *We could never use such stupid arguments again*, Heath noted laconically.[8] Alas, Whitehall then, and from my experience as a minister, now, has mountains of reasons to explain why something should not be done. Democratic government puts ministers into place to explain to state administrators why something should be done. In the British system, unless the Prime Minister is committed to a policy Whitehall caution and orthodoxy – 'whatever best administered is best', to quote Pope – always prevails over ministerial innovation and desire for change.

'The Europeanisation of the Conservative Party is nothing but imperialism with an inferiority complex.'

DENIS HEALEY

A minister can ignore a civil servant's objections if he is confident of having the support of his colleagues and ultimately the Prime Minister. Heath took risks in facing down spurious French demands aimed at spinning out the negotiations to the point where the growing fatigue on the side of both the British and the Six would fatally undermine the chance of agreement. At a meeting with de Gaulle at Macmillan's country home, Birch Grove, in November 1961, Heath discussed in his limited French Britain's application. The French president confessed his puzzlement at how Britain could reconcile its trade and political links with the Commonwealth with full membership of the EEC. But it was not the Commonwealth that led to the collapse of Heath's 18 months of negotiations. As the negotiations went on into 1962, the political will was seeping out of Britain's commitment. Heath took care to cultivate younger Tory MPs, paying attention to the 1959 intake including clever new Conservative MPs like Nicholas Ridley and Eden's former political secretary Peter Tapsell, who were then strong Europhiles. Across the floor of the House the Labour Party had moved to out-and-out opposition. Hugh Gaitskell, the Labour leader, said to join the EEC would 'mean the end of Britain as an independent nation state ... It means the end of a thousand years of history'[9] and was cheered and cheered at the Labour Party conference, which loved such nationalist populism. Harold Wilson, Labour chairman in 1962, said that Gaitskell's 'historic speech' should be printed and sent to every Labour Party member. Denis Healey agreed telling the Labour delegates 'The Europeanisation of the Conservative Party is nothing but imperialism with an inferiority complex.'[10] Labour MPs like the deputy leader, George Brown, and the rising Notting Hill Labourist, Roy Jenkins, were unhappy but to little avail. For Gaitskell, the priority was to unite Labour's left and right, against a Macmillan who had lost the 'Supermac' touch and was beginning to look defeatable. Unlike Nato, which has always enjoyed broad cross-party support, Europe has constantly been used by different factions within both the main British parties to whip up enthusiasms, pander to press proprietors, and throw a political bone to opponents.

Heath had become popular with the top mandarins and diplomats who formed his negotiating team, who admire a minister who can soak up paper, master briefs and deal in detail with foreigners without losing the thread. The Brussels-based press was carefully cultivated. But British journalists covering the EEC had long gone native. To pro-Europeans in business and Britain's opinion-forming classes it looked as if Britain had, at last, a minister who really believed in Europe and was working hard and with success to bring Britain into the EEC.

In fact, by any measurement of political achievement, Heath's negotiations were a success. He had delivered on many technical aspects of the terms of a putative British entry into the EEC. Events however were not so helpful. At the end of 1962, Macmillan had to ask the US permission to buy an off-the-American-shelf nuclear weapons system – the Polaris submarine and its missiles. The Royal Navy would crew the submarines but around the world went the signal that Britain now was locked in with American defence matériel and was not willing to spend the money to develop a truly autonomous and independent defence profile. Britain had little choice. For de Gaulle, still living with the memory of Churchill's famous reply to the French leader in the war – 'If Britain ever has to choose between the continent and the oceans we will always choose the oceans' – it was the end of hopes that Britain and France would come together to create a defence profile that would be independent of all other super-powers. Books have been written on de Gaulle's motives. The British ambassador in Paris had warned Macmillan months previously that de Gaulle would find an excuse for a veto. His warning was dismissed by Macmillan as 'unbelievable'. For many the nuclear weapons issue lay at the heart of de Gaulle's rejection of the British application to join Europe. Heath himself devotes three convoluted pages in his memoirs trying to work his way through the nuclear arms issue as it arose at the end of 1962.[11] Professor John Young also argues de Gaulle hoped for 'co-operation with Britain on nuclear weapons –

the surest way to boost France's international status',[12] while Andrew Roth, writing closer to the events and with an encyclopedic cuttings file and many interviews with the principals, concluded that Macmillan's Polaris agreement with Kennedy 'hardened the French president's belief that Britain was only an American "Trojan Horse"'.[13] John Campbell, Heath's biographer, confirms the orthodox version of British historiography of the events leading to the French veto. 'What, it appears, de Gaulle wanted all along from Britain was a promise of nuclear cooperation, sharing Britain's more advanced nuclear technology. This was the key that might have persuaded the General to allow Britain into Europe.'[14]

By the end of 1962 de Gaulle had won an important referendum that autumn confirming the move to an executive presidency and had obtained a clear majority for his followers in the national assembly. The Algerian imbroglio was on its way to being solved. The British application for entry into Europe, by contrast, was seen as a move to give some life and élan to a tired Conservative government. De Gaulle's focus was Germany and ending

'The French and the Germans have to become brothers ... Folk still see Germany as the hereditary enemy. In reality, the Germans have been our enemies only since 1870 ... Our greatest hereditary enemy was not Germany: it was England. From the Hundred Years War to Fashoda [the squabble between France and Britain over African possessions at the end of the 19th century] Britain has always fought against us. And since then Britain cannot avoid setting her interest against ours. England left us in the lurch at Dunkirk. They happily bombed our fleet at Mers-el-Kébir. They betrayed us in Syria. They always make common cause with America. They want to prevent the successful development of the Common Market.' De Gaulle.[15]

forever the threat to France that a powerful Germany might again pose. Germany was of course divided but de Gaulle knew that the Soviet division of Europe was ahistorical and would not last. Macmillan's game of grandmother's footsteps with Washington and Paris was trivial by comparison. De Gaulle had now to consolidate the EEC to ensure firstly that the wealth Germany gained from a common market for its industrial products would be balanced by the wealth France needed to modernise its agricultural economy. A nuclear alliance with Britain, moreover one that seemed to decouple America from its main west European partner, even were it possible, would have raised every alarm in Germany.

But de Gaulle went further. His chief spokesman, the minister, Alain Peyrefitte, to whom the French leader spoke freely in private kept a careful record of all the General's comments. In June 1962 de Gaulle made clear that his number one strategic objective was reconciliation with Germany. As Heath was busying himself with negotiations, de Gaulle had nothing but contempt for Macmillan's position. 'England [de Gaulle like most Frenchmen uses the term *L'Angleterre* for the United Kingdom] has become an American satellite … As to the Netherlands, the Scandinavians, and all the rest of them, they are satellites of Britain. They are Russian dolls. All these pretty people don't like us and detest our policy.'[16] De Gaulle made clear to Peyrefitte before Macmillan went to his meeting in the Bahamas in December 1962 with Kennedy that he had decided to veto Britain's bid.

What is remarkable was the low level of intelligence in the British political class, including Heath, that no-one sensed, other than the poor British ambassador in Paris whose warnings were dismissed by Macmillan, that France had no interest in agreeing to the efforts Heath was making to negotiate an entry of Britain into the EEC. Heath surrounded himself with French speakers but not French understanders. De Gaulle told Peyrefitte that he had decided 'to shut the Common Market's door to British because they are not ready to enter in economic terms nor are they really ready politically ... I told Macmillan six months ago, then a fortnight ago [22 December 1962] that he had to stop being dependent on the Americans. He told me that is what he wanted as did young people [in Britain]. But he fell into the American trap. Britain is just an American satellite. If they come into the Common Market, Britain will be the Trojan Horse of the Americans. And that means Europe will give up her independence.' Peyrefitte asked de Gaulle if he would use this language at the press conference on 14 January 1963 when he was scheduled to pronounce on the British application. 'Not quite the same words', replied de Gaulle laconically.[17]

Nonetheless de Gaulle was blunt in his veto. If Britain were to join the EEC it would be transformed into 'a colossal Atlantic Community, dependent on America, and directed by America'. It was not about economics. For de Gaulle, states, independent of the reasons they may formally announce, have a deeper organic reasoning process that rational men and their analyses do not understand. Britain's desire to join with Europe was political and would oblige France to share power at a time when France was not ready to dilute its authority within the EEC and Britain was not ready to declare itself a European nation. Other EEC countries which wanted Britain to join and ministers who had admired the diligent, professional way Heath had led the negotiations were disappointed at de Gaulle's veto. But the real moment had been lost in 1950 or at Messina in 1956 when respectively Labour and Conservative ministers refused to chance to enter on the ground floor. By 1962 Britain had to climb higher, offer more, and do so publicly. Macmillan was tired and the Conservatives running out of steam. Shortly after snubbing Britain, de Gaulle and the German Chancellor, Konrad Adenaur signed the Franco-German Treaty which created a core within the EEC. Europe, it appeared, did not need Britain as much as Britain thought.

Heath kept his disappointment under control. Before leaving Brussels he launched a new appeal. *We are part of Europe, by geography, history, culture, tradition and civilisation ... We in Britain are not going to turn our backs on the mainland of Europe, or the countries of the Community.*[18] This was not the prose that any diplomat or mandarin would write for a minister. This was Heath speaking from his heart. He returned to British politics with praise from all sides. The British love a gallant loser who has done his best, offered his all. He was awarded the Charlemagne Prize by Aachen, the city where Charlemagne is buried, and used the money to buy a Steinway grand piano. Heath had left the ranks of cabinet ministers who are competent administrators and a safe pair of hands with the media or in the Commons. Heath's efforts to take Britain into Europe made him into a serious, heavyweight political player – loathed by the anti-Europeans, admired by the pro-Europeans.

As always, Heath had kept in with the older generation of Tory leaders. When Macmillan stepped down as a result of his prostate condition in the autumn of 1963, Heath supported his chief in the foreign office, Lord Home, who disclaimed his title and led the Conservatives to their election defeat in October 1964. In the short premiership of Sir Alec Douglas-Home, as the aristocrat had now become, Heath became

We are part of Europe, by geography, history, culture, tradition and civilisation ... We in Britain are not going to turn our backs on the mainland of Europe, or the countries of the Community.

HEATH

President of the Board of Trade and moved to liberalise the retail sector by making it illegal for manufacturers to decide the prices at which goods should be sold in shops. Such an elementary piece of competitive economics might have been thought to command support from a right-wing party. It was the norm in the United States and under EEC rules it was illegal for such price-rigging which meant no new retailer could arrive and offer to sell goods more cheaply to attract more customers. Heath underestimated the deep longing in his own party for protectionist economics and the belief that too much competition was dangerous to a settled stability in a nation. More than 40 Tory MPs refused to support the second reading of the bill aimed at abolishing these price cartels. What was logical and necessary to Heath required political coaxing for Tory MPs. Napoleon's jibe that Britain was a nation of shopkeepers came to life as retailers, frightened of competition, told their MPs to prevent Heath pushing through his competitive reforms on behalf of consumers without money in their pockets to pay the higher prices the price-rigging cartels wanted to impose.

Heath took control of the Policy Advisory Committee and unlike the polite, *noblesse oblige* border Scot he was willing to use rough language attacking Labour ministers. He became Shadow Chancellor, while the rival for the post-Home Tory party of his generation, Reginald Maudling, became Shadow Foreign Secretary, which is a nice post for travel but rarely allows its occupant to shine in the Commons. Maudling kept lucrative outside directorships. Out of office, Heath's hard-working style meant he was always well-prepared. He tabled 1,222 amendments to Labour's first budget and in three divisions won the vote. Never had an incoming government been so mercilessly harried. Heath, still without family or much outside life save his music, was available at all hours in the Commons where he felt at home and where MPs, who now had the power to elect the Leader of the Conservative Party, came to admire, if not warm to, this utterly committed political animal. Alec Douglas-Home sloughed off the leadership of the Conservative Party as he was soon to shrug off his brief foray into being a commoner. In July 1965, Heath entered the contest against Maudling from the Tory left and Powell, already identified as an unflinching rightist. Maudling was a calm communicator, comfortable in his skin, and so middle-of-the-road that it was impossible to dislike Reggie. But it was MPs not the public or Tory Party members who would decide. The election was not so clear cut. Heath got 150 votes, Maudling 133 and Powell 15. So Heath had just scraped over the 50 per cent mark. It was enough to make him party leader. But he inherited a party in which half its MPs did not want him.

Chapter 6: Taking on Wilson

Having won the backing of just half of Conservative MPs, Heath went on to lose the first of three elections he led the Tory Party into. He could not be blamed for the 1966 defeat. The British voters were impressed by the no-nonsense Yorkshire grittiness of Harold Wilson, and avuncular right-wing Jim Callaghan at the Treasury showed this was not an adventurous government. But it was, at last, moving with the times as the death penalty was abolished and laws promoting social reform giving men and women rights to decide for themselves about their sexuality and fertility were proposed. In the many histories of the politics of the time or biographies of Conservative leaders, few, if any, discuss the *Zeitgeist* problem. I went up to Oxford in 1966 and it was little changed from the Oxford Ted Heath and Harold Wilson attended. Eating in Hall was obligatory. Wearing gowns was compulsory. The college doors were shut and locked at midnight. Drinking heavily was excused but being caught with drugs or a girl in your room meant expulsion. By the time I left on the eve of Heath becoming Prime Minister, Oxford was utterly changed. The porter sold marijuana, the doors to the college never shut, you could sleep with whom you liked where you liked and how you liked, the university administration buildings had been occupied and the reforming Labour Prime Minister of 1964 had become uniformly loathed. Wilson's growing unpopularity did not translate into greater personal appeal for Heath amongst the 1968 generation. His image was of a man who wanted to recreate the 1950s with its pre-Beatles, pre-Stones, pre-sex, pre-hash stuffy conformities.

It is a lucky political leader and prime minister who can be instinctively not just in tune with the time but help to make the way voters see the world that they think the times are in tune with the prime minister they have elected. Margaret Thatcher and Tony Blair shared that quality, as did to a lesser extent Attlee and Macmillan. Wilson had it for a brief period, perhaps three years after winning power in 1964. But Heath never had such luck. His politics was one of perspiration not inspiration, good management and organisation, not brilliant oratory. As the British Empire faded into history books, Heath was faced with intractable left-overs from the heritage of white British occupation and denial over centuries and decades of core human rights like self-governance. Rhodesia was one such problem. Another was black African racism and Islamophobia, as first the Kenyan and then the Ugandan governments turned their Asian populations into homeless asylum seekers all looking to the mother

Today, Heath's sporting achievements as a world-class yachtsman and his musical gifts would win admirers. In the late 1960s they seemed a little odd. The British like messing about on boats, not throwing oneself into a yacht to turn it, a crew and yourself into world beaters. Tinkling on the ivories is always popular, but there was something earnest, almost un-English, in the way Heath took his music so portentously. When he became leader of the Conservative Party, the anatomist of Britain, Anthony Sampson described him thus: 'Heath has a blank, boyish face, smooth grey hair, an intense manner which gives way suddenly and disconcertingly to a bright smile and shaking laughter.'[1]

country, Britain for a home. Heath as Leader of the Opposition and later Prime Minister had to deal with another British colonial left-over – the question of Palestine as Arab nationalists sought to uproot the Jewish people from their tiny nation on its contested parcel of land. India and Pakistan fought a war and Pakistan was split in half as the eastern part of the Muslim nation turned itself into Bangladesh.

Heath was not interested in imperial nostalgia. He loathed racism, and he wanted Britain to become a modern European nation. But he had his party and the 150 Conservative MPs who did not vote for him to worry about. Unity in the Shadow Cabinet, in the parliamentary party, in the broader party at large with its strong presence in Scotland and northern and midlands town halls was Heath's main priority. Yet the leader for whom unity predominates, is the leader who ends up unsure how to lead. Heath had to include everyone in his Shadow Cabinet – the laid-back, old-fashioned Border Scot aristocrat Alec Douglas-Home, the unbending Brummie ideologue Enoch Powell whose logic never worried about plunging over precipices, the lazily venal Reginald Maudling, and the cerebral Iain Macleod, condemned by the Tory grandee Lord Salisbury as 'too clever by half' – a remark no-one would make about the earnest Edward Heath. A founder member of the One Nation group had been Angus Maude. He was Shadow Colonial Secretary but this did not prevent him appealing for a return to old Toryism with its explicit rebuke of Heath's modernisation strategy. His appeal for a more common, populist touch in an article early in 1966 in the *Spectator*, then as now the magazine that defines much contemporary politics, argued 'The Conservative Party has completely lost effective political initiative. Its own supporters in the country are divided and deeply worried by this failure ... For the Tories simply to talk like technocrats will get them nowhere.'[2] In the television contest with Harold Wilson, Heath was outclassed. Anthony Wedgewood Benn, as he then was, noted in his diary on 3 November 1965: 'To Number 10 in the evening to hear Ted Heath doing a TV broadcast. He was odiously ingratiating and the programme had begun with the applause after his speech at the Tory conference, and had shown pictures of him sitting and smirking. He only made two firm points, one anti-trade union and the other attacking us for failing to help the owner-occupier. But he ended by saying. *"The difference between the socialists and ourselves is that they believe in the State and we believe in the family."* Whether this was intended to draw attention away from his own bachelor status or was meant seriously, it didn't go down well.'[3]

To be fair, there was little that Heath could do or have done to stop the decision of British voters to give Labour a working majority – of 97 – in the general election of March 1966. That followed by England's World Cup victory and Wilson's gimmick of bestowing MBEs on the Beatles left the Labour Prime Minister dominant on the British media stage. No politician or political party likes to lose an election. Some elections are good to lose because the party has not renewed itself sufficiently – Labour in 1992 is a recent example, but in 1966, the tag of loser hung around Heath's neck but the rupture with the Macmillan-Home Tory era had taken place. Heath could embark on fashioning a new Conservatism. How far did he succeed? Not yet 50, the first thing he did was bring down the age of the Shadow Cabinet and bring in more meritocratic, grammar school MPs like Peter Walker, Anthony Barber, Robert Carr, Geoffrey Rippon and Margaret Thatcher. Jim Prior was Heath's Parliamentary Private Secretary, 1965–70, and recalls being asked who might be, in Prior's vocabulary, the 'statutory woman' and suggested Thatcher's name to Heath. 'There was a long silence. "Yes," he said, "Willie (Whitelaw⟩ agrees she's much the most able, but he says that once she's there we'll never be able to get rid of her."'[4] A word of caution is needed in this play between grammar and public school. The new Tories might better be defined as self-made. Birth had given them no advantage. They had had to buy their own furniture, not inherit land, houses and paintings, but many like Margaret Thatcher married wealth and adopted the accent and style of old Tories.

Heath could not go all the way in changing the party profile. After all, he had risen to the top by being the loyal aide to the old Tories. He adopted their clothes, was welcome as an unencumbered bachelor at their dinners and country weekends, tried unsuccessfully to speak like them, and in his new duplex flat in the Albany, the favourite apartment block for a London *pied à terre* for the upper classes, which he had decorated in best Knightsbridge out of Peter Jones style, Heath seemed to want to be an old-style Tory. Might Heath have adopted a modernisation strategy copied from the Continent? First the planners under the Fourth Republic and then de Gaulle with a regal hauteur had ruthlessly modernised France, bringing electricity and good roads to every corner of a country two-and-half times the size of Britain. Having cut the Algerian Gordian knot, de Gaulle imposed a strong money policy not dissimilar to that urged by the Powellites as the only way of curbing inflation and forcing managers to improve productivity or find themselves without the capital necessary to improve or even survive their business. David Butler, the Oxford political scientist, interviewed Heath in April 1965 and noted that Heath 'despairs of the efficiency, enterprise of British industry … he is most worried of all about the machinery of government and thirsts after a Gaullist solution.'

The independent central bank in Germany forced similar monetary discipline on German ministers. In Britain, a Chancellor could play fast and loose with interest rates and money supply. Labour was caught out when in 1967, as in 1976, the weakness of sterling obliged bending to international money markets. Devaluation in the fixed exchange rate system of Bretton Woods was a coherent policy option. But the Wilson government might have devalued of its own free will in 1964 – much as Labour achieved a tremendous boost by copying the rest of Europe and allowing the UK central bank to set interest rates after 1997 – but when the devaluation was forced on Wilson in 1967 it looked like an imposed humiliation. British citizens were only allowed to take £50 out of Britain for their holidays in Europe. The amount was stamped in the back of a passport rather as if they were naughty children for wanting to take their vacations in France. Everyone found ways around this ridiculous rule. For Wilson who had a holiday home in the Scilly Isles or Callaghan who thought the Isle of Wight was sufficiently offshore these petty regulations had no impact. For the millions of middle and working class Britons who were discovering the pleasure of cheap drinks, cigarettes and endless sun in Spain and Italy and Greece, the exchange control rules were a reminder of how provincial and out-of-touch Labour ministers were.

British politicians also looked to the Nordic countries for inspiration. The Swedish concept of the Ombudsman was introduced. But social democracy in Scandinavia was based on a ruthless modernisation aimed at making local and national capitalism able to compete in any world market. Their trade unions had long since removed any trace of Communist or militant shop steward behaviour. Taxes were high but raised and spent locally. Elections were decided on the proportion of national votes cast, not fought constituency by constituency on a first-past-the-post basis as in Britain. To even begin moving Britain towards a more Nordic model of government and management of the economy and society would have required an unprecedented modernisation of the state, as well as of business and unions. Heath was a Conservative. He wanted to reform Britain but he presided over a party that did not like reform. The writer Evelyn Waugh lamented that no post-war Tory government had managed to turn the clock back one little bit. Hindsight suggests that Heath was more at ease with Continental Christian Democracy than with British Conservatism with its roots in squires and shires, and an automatic legislative majority in the second chamber of the UK parliament thanks to the notion that Britain's laws should be decided on account of a legislator's birth to an aristocrat. To re-invent wholesale a political party with the historical weight and roots of the British Conservatives was a mammoth undertaking. It requires defeat after defeat and a lengthy period out of power before a party is ready to renew itself. The Tories saw Labour as a temporary power-holding phenomenon. Like Attlee after 1945, the best Labour would do is a few years in office and then internal party divisions as well as economic reality would deliver the nation back to its natural rulers – the Conservatives. Thus for Heath there was not any real pressure to recast his own party in the late 1960s.

Heath did venture into constitutional reform when he suggested more devolved rule to Scotland and even a Scottish parliament. As a result Scottish Tories kept winning seats for a generation to come though it would take a further three decades before any constitutional modernisation was enacted. Heath tentatively supported reform of the House of Lords but faced with the parliamentary opposition of the deeply romantic conservatives Enoch Powell and Michael Foot, he was not willing to help the ailing Labour premier in his bid at modernising Parliament. For the most part, Heath allowed the Wilson government to come apart at its economic seams. The devaluation of 1967 did not bring about the desired benefits. George Brown's National Economic Plan turned out to be little more than paper and when the Labour deputy leader moved to the Foreign Office he turned into an embarrassment as he wandered from diplomatic reception to diplomatic reception often seriously the worse for wear from drink. The Labour government had little idea what to do with trade unions which refused all appeals for modernisation. Wilson had tried to incorporate unions into a broader Labour programme and offered Frank Cousin, the leader of the biggest union, the Transport and General Workers Union, a minister's job. It did not work. The TUC tried to police wage agreements on a voluntary basis but to no avail. Young militant trade unionists were gaining in influence in the unions. One of them, John Prescott, helped organise a seven week-long seamen's strike in the summer of 1966, cutting UK trade with the world. Later as a senior Labour minister Mr Prescott became the hammer of ideological militancy directed at a Labour government. In 1966, there was no one inside the trade unions who could control him.

Wilson was forced to impose wage controls in 1966 and spent the rest of his administration against a background of mounting working class discontent opposed to statutory incomes policy. As the trade union historian Robert Taylor has written national incomes policy was rejected by the trade unions. 'It had not been used to bring about any redistribution of income, help the low paid or provide an opportunity for genuine productivity bargaining.'[5] Labour's income taxes and other indirect taxes used to pay for improved public services fell disproportionately on the lower paid. In

1960, the average male manual worker paid 8 per cent of his income in tax and national insurance. By 1970, this had risen to 20 per cent. Workers moved from the decade of 'you've never had it so good' to the decade of never being so highly taxed. Whatever nominal wage increases workers did obtain resulted in only a tiny increase in real income as deductions took their toll. In elections in Britain's great cities, where the working class predominated, the Tories made gain after gain. Yet despite the failure of incomes policy, Heath drew no intellectual or policy conclusions in direction of an alternative practice were the Conservatives to win power. In March 1968, Heath announced *I am quite prepared for a tough incomes policy to ensure costs do not outrun productivity.* By the time of the 1970 election manifesto he appeared to have changed his mind as the Tory manifesto, *A Better Tomorrow*, stated: 'We utterly reject the philosophy of compulsory wage control.' In fact, Heath simply refused to work through the philosophy or the practice of what should be the relationship between prices, incomes and output in a market economy. It would cost him dear and make the 1970s a wasted decade for Britain.

Instead Heath looked to legal reforms of how trade unions operated to turn labour market relations away from the zero-sum game they became under Labour. The 1966 Conservative manifesto proposed legally binding agreements, the registration of unions, and industrial courts to make judgements on workplace disputes. In sum, this became the law as passed in the Industrial Relations Act of 1971 which gave rise to first a guerrilla and then an all-out war between the trade unions and the Heath government. Other countries had developed trade union practice without such legislation. In Germany, trade unions did not seek individual agreements with companies. Instead, regional wage deals were shaped and accepted on a voluntary basis. German unions had their own rules which required three-quarters of members to vote in secret before a strike could start. German employees and union representative on the boards of big companies and worked collaboratively to improve profits and productivity. But in Germany, as in Sweden, or the United States, there was a system of industrial unionism which meant all workers in a given industry and workplace were organised and represented by just one union. In Britain, in the print and car industries alone there would be as many as a dozen trade unions each organising the membership of a small group of workers but each with its own distinct needs and levels of militancy. Above all, in continental Europe and in North America, unions controlled their workplace activists. In Britain, shop stewards controlled unions especially as a new generation of left-wing union leaders, like Jack Jones and Hugh Scanlan, rose on the basis of the support they won from the shop stewards.

Wilson tried his own attempts at reforming the unions by legislative means when the Employment Secretary, Barbara Castle, published her white paper, *In Place of Strife*, in 1969. It was opposed by the unions and, more ominously, by Labour grandees like James Callaghan. It came too late and was seen as a panic response to increased trade union anger over wage controls and a reactionary employer class indifferent to partnership with workers. Heath had a strategic choice to make. Although *In Place of Strife* did not go as far as Tory proposals it was a major step forward in inviting the unions to modernise themselves. Jim Prior, who took a keen interest in employment affairs, argued that Heath should have welcomed the Labour reform proposals as a move toward Conservative thinking. Such a move, argued Prior, 'would have done wonders for the country and still left the Labour Party seething with discontent. I believe Ted ... should have spotted the opportunity.'[6] Instead the Tories went in for short-term tactics of dismissing the Castle proposals and promising to oppose them in Parliament. Two years later, Labour returned the compliment by an equally opportunistic root-and-branch opposition to Heath's trade union reforms.

Heath had an increasingly acerbic and personal relationship with Wilson. In the Commons, Wilson was the master. Heath was unable to score many points. When Heath urged cooperation with the French, Wilson baited him by saying the Tory leader was 'rolling over like a spaniel' to support de Gaulle. Heath responded with fury at Wilson's jibe. *This is too sordid for words ... Wilson must be out of his mind ... Abuse like this is unforgiveable when you are dealing with international relations.*[7] When Wilson suggested that Heath had acted improperly in sending someone to Salisbury to talk to the racist Smith regime, Heath snapped back: *If Mr Wilson considers that any offence has been committed by Her Majesty's Opposition, or that there has been any breach of the Official Secrets Act, let him prosecute me and my colleagues forthwith. If not, let him shut up. There are no lessons to be learnt in patriotism from Mr Wilson.* Heath described Wilson's price and incomes policy as seeking to put in place a *totalitarian society.* In one exchange in the Commons, the feisty Labour veteran, Manny Shinwell, rose and asked 'Is this a private row or can I join in?'[8] According to Harold Wilson 'For three years I had to put up with sustained personal attacks in almost every speech Mr Heath [made].'[9]

Although Heath had suggested defence cooperation with the French and hinted at the possibility of a Franco-British nuclear arms arrangement in a 1965 lecture, he did not take forward the idea. On the contrary, when Wilson began to dissociate the Labour government from the US bombing of

Wilson must be out of his mind ... Abuse like this is unforgivable when you are dealing with international relations.

HEATH

North Vietnam, Heath rushed to the defence of President Johnson and attacked Wilson. Heath was rewarded with a lengthy talk with Johnson in the White House. It helped keep the pro-American wing of the Tories happy but further alienated young people and the large number of students at the new universities which had opened in the 1960s. Heath could afford to ignore student unrest. While students marched, demonstrated and occupied, the broader mass of the population in Britain and abroad looked askance at the behaviour of a generation who had been sent to study at taxpayers' expense and used their grants to oppose everything their parents stood for. In France and the United States, the right easily won elections as the hundreds of thousands of students on campuses were outweighed by the millions of voters who thought students should study, not revolt.

The Conservatives were torn between the efforts of Heath to make the party more modern and the obligations of adversarial politics in the Commons and in the media which expect strident opposition to the government of the day. An absurd discussion of a possible coup organised by the vain, self-important newspaper chief, Cecil King, revealed the extent of febrility in parts of the British establishment. After Rhodesia where Tory right-wingers despised what they considered Heath's pusillanimity came the decision to send the British Army onto the streets of Belfast and Derry. Suddenly part of the United Kingdom looked more like the southern American states during the civil rights conflicts. Heath came under pressure from backbenchers to be more robust in support of protestant supremacists in Ulster. Wilson had made an unsuccessful bid to join the EEC and was snubbed by de Gaulle much as Macmillan and Heath had been. However this defeat for Wilson did not help Heath. As he told the Oxford don, David Butler, in November 1969, *Europe has become much more difficult because Wilson has taken it over as his own issue. Therefore people in the party who were willing to go along with the European policy while it was being followed by Macmillan, have turned against it.*[10]

Immigration was also a problem. The arrival of scores of thousands of Commonwealth citizens in the previous two decades changed the face of many poorer British suburbs. They brought in family members, settled, and communities grew which had a different identity from the existing population which had to share space, housing, and welfare benefits with new people who had different languages, religions, cultures and behaviour patterns from existing communities. Race riots had broken out in West London and were whipped up by an ageing Oswald Mosley. Patrick Gordon Walker, Labour Shadow Foreign Secretary, lost his West Midlands seat in 1964 when the Conservative candidate campaigned under the slogan, 'If You Want a Nigger Neighbour – Vote Labour'. Many on the right of the Tory Party were racist, and they found a hero in Enoch Powell who made speeches on immigrants and against the Labour government's decision to admit to Britain Asians expelled by the racist black government of Kenya. (Powell's politics on race and his infamous 'rivers of blood' speech are discussed in Chapter 11 as Enoch Powell was Heath's nemesis.) In a dramatic move in April 1968 Heath dismissed Powell from the Shadow Cabinet following his speech which set alight racial tension in Britain as had never been seen before. Heath's decision to fire Powell was seen as tough leadership and welcomed by the liberal establishment and especially the press. But many backbench MPs and party activists were closer to Powell than to Heath on immigration and race.

In the end, Harold Wilson helped to make Heath appear as a no-nonsense right-wing Conservative leader when he mocked the Shadow Cabinet seminar held in the winter of 1970. In best modern management style, Heath took his putative ministers as well as Tory research staff and policy experts for an away day to a hotel, Selsdon Park, near Croydon – the kind of seat the Tories had to win in order to form a government. Peter Walker recalls that on the second day, Saturday, of the conference, Heath was told that he would have to give a news conference at midday to provide fodder for the Sunday papers. 'But,' says Walker, 'we hadn't actually done much work or come to any real conclusions. Ted asked "What on earth do I tell the journalists?" Iain Macleod said, "Just tell them we are keen on law and order, Ted." Thus Selsdon Man was born.'[11] Heath announced that the Conservative priorities in office would be tax cuts, union reform, immigration control; law and order with a new law on trespass that would stop the anti-apartheid demonstration which had disrupted the Springboks rugby and cricket tours, and more money for pensioners aged over 80.

Wilson denounced what he called 'Selsdon Man [which] is not just a lurch to the right, it is an atavistic desire to reverse the course of 25 years of social revolution. What they are panning is a wanton, calculated and deliberate return to greater inequality.'[12] This was precisely the language that Tory activists and hard-line supporters wanted to hear. Wilson's attack gave the Conservatives something Heath had not been able to provide as he zigzagged over the policy challenges thrown up in the 1960s. 'Selsdon Man' might have been appropriate to apply to Enoch Powell and other right-wing Tories but it was not where the managerial One Nation Heath was. Wilson had lost the support of those tired of incomes policy, his failure to reform trade unions, and his inability to make progress on Rhodesia, Ireland, or Europe. There was also a nastier, resentful Britain spread across class and wealth divides which disliked the arrival, *en masse*, of immigrants from the Asian and Caribbean Commonwealth. They were ready to come out for a man who appeared to promise a rupture with the way Britain was run, even though Heath himself was, in his own way, as much a centrist and anti-racist and more of a moderniser than Wilson.

Wilson called an election for June 1970. I was starting as a reporter for the BBC in Birmingham then and it was clear to me that no-one was inspired by Labour. It was not that voters liked Heath. But they were no longer enthused, inspired, or convinced by Wilson. When, at Euston Station, coming back to Birmingham having worked a Sunday shift on the *Daily Mirror*, I heard that England had been eliminated by Germany from the World Cup I knew instinctively that it was curtains for Wilson. David Butler observed Heath on the campaign trail. 'He said he came with a "simple three word message; We are winning". At subsequent stops this became a simple two word message "We're winning."'[13] Despite opinion polls putting Wilson ahead and a sense of defeat in many top Tory leaders, Heath plugged away. His victory was solid enough. He won 46 per cent of the vote to Labour's 43 per cent. The Conservatives won 77 seats. Labour's huge 1966 majority simply evaporated. A disunited party does not get re-elected. With 330 Conservative seats to Labour's 287 Heath had a clear majority in the Commons. At a victory celebration a few weeks after he became Prime Minister, Heath rounded on David Butler. *We did win the election you know, we did. You people are so obsessed with the idea that Harold Wilson*

We did win the election you know, we did. You people are so obsessed with the idea that Harold Wilson can't do anything wrong and I can't do anything right, that you don't realise we won the election.

HEATH

can't do anything wrong and I can't do anything right, that you don't realise we won the election.[14]

Part Two

THE LEADERSHIP

Chapter 7: Downing Street Years

Heath set out to change the tone of government after his victory over Harold Wilson. He told the Tories at their victory conference, *We will have to embark on a change so radical, a revolution so quiet and yet so total that it will go far beyond the programme for a Parliament.*[1] The win was very much his own achievement, as opinion polls, press commentators and Heath's own lacklustre performance in the Commons had combined to create a climate of opinion which saw Heath as a loser. Now he was in command of Downing Street and he owed no-one a debt for his victory. 'Today, with his "comfortable" yet compact figure, a good and usually sun-tanned colour, clear blue eyes and strong grey hair, he looks just what he is – a man of middle years in excellent physical condition. He stands 5ft 10½in. and he weighs, in his own words, 165 lb' is how Heath was described in 1970.[2] A few months previously he had won an international yacht race between Australia and Tasmania. Heath would be at the helm of government with every member of his crew ready to jump to his orders. The navigation and helmsmanship was impressive but where did Heath want to steer Britain?

An easy answer might be modernisation. But this would challenge the deeper atavistic Conservatism of the party he led. It would have required a philosophy, a sense of a new narrative that would make the British see their country in a different way and agree to overcome resistance to reform to achieve that modernisation. Instead of modernisation, Heath opted for management. Well worked-out decisions would solve Britain's many problems. Campaigning to win power, famously, is poetry; government is prose. Heath, despite being the most cultured Prime Minister of the 20th century with a huge musical knowledge, a proper acquaintance with painting, especially French Impressionists, and high standards in decoration which he used to turn 10 Downing Street and Chequers into lighter, airy, flower-filled offices and reception rooms, was never a man of words. Few political leaders are, but they can hire word managers to write inspiring prose or find a single phrase or metaphor that instils itself in people's minds. Heath, the skipper and conductor, refused to have an effective team around him in Downing Street.

He remained a loner. When he came to dine as an Honorary Fellow to Nuffield College, Oxford in March 1971, he talked about negotiations in Brussels and talks in Singapore in which there was only one central figure – himself. David Butler, a fellow of Nuffield, noted, 'It was a very Wilsonian sort of egocentricity and it was quite easy to reinterpret the anecdotes in a very different way from the point of view of the victims of Heath's self-imputed brilliance.'[3] Butler later discussed Heath as Prime Minister with Sir William Armstrong, head of the civil service, who observed 'It's a terrible office. Everything is done to feed your ego ... At the moment there is almost nobody who speaks up to him. I am told that this or that can't be done because Ted's against it. I ask why they say "Oh, he said something

We will have to embark on a change so radical, a revolution so quiet and yet so total that it will go far beyond the programme for a Parliament.

HEATH

during the election or three months ago". I suggest they should argue it again with him, but they are frightened to. In fact, he is much more amenable to reason than many people think, although he is very deeply taken with the idea that the time for words is passed. Action is what is needed. It is quite convenient, of course, if you want something done, you dress it up as action and get it authorised.' Heath no longer had more senior figures to look up to like Churchill, Macmillan or even Douglas-Home. His Cabinet had no strong personalities once Iain Macleod died very soon after taking office and Quintin Hogg was restored to the House of Lords as Lord Chancellor.

He had just one woman – Margaret Thatcher – in his Cabinet. 1970 was a year when feminism moved from theory to a mass movement of emancipation. Heath loved women's company, especially that of those who were musically literate, and in his quest for good decoration and stylish soirées at Downing Street, there was a feminine side to the new Prime Minister. Yet Heath had a wooden ear for the new movements which were changing Britain's society at an accelerating pace. He did not think to deliberately promote women or find space for the young professionals beginning to emerge from Britain's ethnic communities. He remained wedded to Macmillan's social Conservatism based on Keynesian economic theory. But, the application of Keynesianism to one country, Britain, was based on a closed economy sheltered behind traditional trading and currency arrangements. By 1970 this no longer worked. As David Marquand has written: 'Policy-makers were trapped in an impasse from which Keynesian[ism] ... could offer no escape. The result was a crisis of confidence and belief, more disorientating than the economic crisis which had given rise to it.'[4] In 1970, Heath had handsomely and decisively beaten Labour. It was not the policies that needed changing so much as the politics and the politicians. Put a different team into ministries and the policies by which Britain had been governed since 1945 could be made to work.

Heath had a small group of co-workers like the former diplomat, Douglas Hurd, who had worked as Heath's private secretary since 1967 and the intellectual wordsmith Michael Wolf in Downing Street. The former spent a great deal of time seeking to find a seat himself – an endless, time-consuming business. One of the most important aides a prime minister has is a press officer. Bernard Ingham for Margaret Thatcher and Alistair Campbell for Tony Blair were brilliant news managers with an aggressive political style that allowed their masters to dominate the media. Heath brought in a foreign office diplomat, Donald Maitland, whom he had enjoyed working with when negotiating EEC membership in 1962. Career diplomats are rarely good press officers as John Major discovered when he appointed the diplomat, Christopher Meyer, to be his press officer and enjoyed media coverage as bad, if not worse, than any other Prime Minister. A press officer has to be of the same political flesh and bones, an extension of his boss. Maitland was a calm professional but believed in the Foreign Office tradition of giving away as little as possible to journalists. A modernising Prime Minister might have seized on the more open style of government in other countries, some already with freedom of information legislation. Heath tried to hold open press conferences – a first for a British Prime Minister – but they were organised in grand pomp in Lancaster House, and looked more like de Gaulle's Olympian presentations to the fawning Paris press than a modern news conference. The experiment did not last.

Instead, Heath, so often described in the past as a perfect permanent under-secretary material, relied on his civil servants. This was a deliberate attempt to break with the

Wilson 'kitchen cabinet' style, with Downing Street full of cronies fighting with Marcia Williams for the Prime Minister's ear. But it left Heath without intimate and close advisers who could tell him hard political truths and steer him away from dead-ends and zero-sum confrontations. Straight away he stumbled over the problem of incomes policy. Municipal, power and postal workers all went on strike in the first months of Heath's government. As employer, the government did not know what to do about meeting the pay demands of staff in the public sector. Commissions were set up to investigate the workers' demands. They usually split the middle with pay increases ahead of inflation which were then used by other unions to demand similar or better wage hikes. Far from moving government away from the commanding heights of the economy, Heath was persuaded to leave the nationalised steel industry and the airlines in state hands. In fact, the first major act of the government was to take Rolls-Royce into public ownership. The alternative was the world-renowned firm going into bankruptcy and closing down. So for the first time since 1949, a major industrial firm was nationalised. Was this why people had voted Conservative? The Tories lost the Conservative seat of Bromsgrove in a by-election in the autumn of 1970. I worked for the successful Labour candidate, Terry Davis. Knocking on West Midlands doors just months after his triumphal entry into Downing Street, it was obvious that Heath did not have much pull with voters.

It did not faze the new Prime Minister. He had enough experience from government in the 1950s and 1960s to know how bad headlines in one period can melt away as government moves on to new areas of policy where leadership can be shown and the nation's core interests promoted. Heath had placated the Tory right by agreeing to sell arms to South Africa. He tried to find agreement with Ian Smith over Rhodesia but the problem was insurmountable given the whites' insistence on minority rule and the black majority wanting nothing less than the chance to live under Robert Mugabe. These foreign problems provoked anger from the liberal-left in Britain but were not first-order priorities.

For Heath there was only one international question that mattered: taking Britain into Europe. Business and most of the media supported EEC entry. Labour was moving firmly in the direction of anti-Europeanism but a large grouping of Labour MPs, including many of the brightest young newly-elected members like John Smith and Philip Whitehead, were strongly pro-European and would vote to support Heath. Three hundred and thirty Conservative MPs appeared to support EEC entry though it was clear from the debates in the Commons during the unsuccessful Wilson application that two or three dozen Tories had latched on to the sovereignty argument and would need persuading to vote to enter Europe. The Beaverbrook press was hostile but the new Australian newspaper tycoon Rupert Murdoch was strongly pro-European. Heath's Cabinet were united in the belief that European entry would be the mechanism that would help modernise British industry and begin the process of raising economic performance, productivity, and management standards to match the better performing economies on the continent. Margaret Thatcher was 'wholeheartedly in favour of British entry into the EEC'.[5]

Heath was staunchly anti-Communist and Britain expelled 105 Russians with diplomatic status in 1971 on suspicion they had been spies. The Soviet Union responded angrily. Heath never went to Moscow or met Soviet leaders as Prime Minister. He also continued the support he had extended in opposition to US policy in south-east Asia and even tried to create a new five-power defence pact in the Far East. But Heath refused to make the early pilgrimage to Washington and it was Nixon who came to Chequers for the first meeting between the two conservative leaders in the English-speaking world. Henry Kissinger, Nixon's foreign policy supremo, was puzzled at Heath's coldness towards America. 'Paradoxically, while the other European leaders strove to improve their relations with us ... Heath went in the opposite direction. His relations with us were always correct, but they rarely rose above a basic reserve that prevented – in the name of Europe – the close co-operation with us that was his for the taking.'[6] Yet from Heath's point of view America invested little in the so-called 'special relationship' – a term Heath refused to use. Nixon abruptly took the US out of the Bretton Woods system of managed currencies in order to allow the dollar to sink, thus damaging UK exports. Moreover, the Americans imposed a 10 per cent surcharge on imports into the US. The US also supported Pakistan against India in the 1971 conflict on the grounds that India was a Soviet satellite at a time when London was closer to New Delhi. And then in the biggest diplomatic coup of the post-war world, Nixon turned up in China, reversing a quarter-century of anti-Chinese hostility. The British Prime Minister got a few hours' notice of the American President's policy volte-face.

In his memoirs, Heath downplays the differences with Nixon which were certainly seen to be acute by contemporary observers. Heath says that Nixon even gave his presidential blessing to Heath's ambition to create an Anglo-French nuclear deterrent. Heath had been worrying at this bone since he became Leader of the Opposition. From his point of view it was a way of drawing France back fully into NATO after de Gaulle's withdrawal from the military (not political) pillar of the alliance. It also meant Britain offering to France the

The Special Relationship

Heath 'made himself into something of a Euro-intellectual … His conviction was clear from 1950, his experience established by 1963. Then, in 1967, he gave shape to his view of the future with a series of lectures at Harvard University…. It prepared the ground for a break not only with Macmillan's priorities – the Atlantic relationship, the Commonwealth – but with the ongoing sensitivities of the Conservative Party…. Heath, in other words was framing a political future for the Community, and the flesh he put on it was fattest in the realm of defence. He harked back to a European defence community, and in the process declared himself, by the standards of post-war convention, a less convinced Atlanticist than any other British leader. He talked up the sacrilegious idea of nuclear pooling between France and Britain, and openly canvassed for *an eventual European defence system.*

This was the working out, in opposition, of new and distinct priorities, while little noticed by the Conservative Party, became disturbing to the Americans. Heath was never anti-American, in the way the Labour left had spent a lifetime being. Yet here was the emergence of a philosophy, a harbinger of his years in power, which foretold a drastic change not only from Macmillan's intimacies with John F Kennedy but from Wilson's cringing submission to Lyndon Johnson. In this, Heath was to remain consistent. Henry Kissinger, in his memoirs, recalled a Prime Minister who dealt "with us with an unsentimentality totally at variance with the *special relationship.*" Unlike other European leaders, who "strove to improve their relations with us … Heath went in the opposite direction". It was a conscious choice, based on the perception that the old concentric circles were no longer quite as equi-cyclical as they were when Churchill talked about them. Europe, in Heath's assessment, had to become the largest: a position that actually gave him much in common, paradoxically, with de Gaulle. From time to time, Heath made speeches that could be called Gaullist, talking about the need to *redress the balance* against the dollar, and speaking with disapproval of *an allegiance foreign to Europe.* [Hugo Young, *This Blessed Plot* (Macmillan, London: 1998) pp 221f.]

concept of European defence and military power projection beyond that permitted by Washington. He told Nixon in December 1970 of his thinking and the US president replied 'You should feel that you have a great deal of running room on this ... if exploratory discussions were to show that the concept of Anglo-French nuclear collaboration could be used for this purpose than it would have American support.'[7] A startled Kissinger spoke to Burke Trend, Heath's Cabinet Secretary, afterwards and begged him not to allow this part of the conversation to become known as American voters would turn against a US president happy to promote a European nuclear bomb, based on Anglo-French nuclear co-operation.[8]

Tensions between Washington and Heath flared again over the attack by Egypt on Israel during the Jewish holy week of Yom Kippur. America sought to prevent the elimination of the Jewish state and promised to send arms to the Israelis. Heath joined with other European nations in refusing the US over-flight rights. It was an irritation rather than a substantial policy move but once inside the EEC, Heath argued that foreign policy positions should be agreed by the Nine. Heath's handling of America remains a puzzle. He had American friends and had matured as a politician working closely with Churchill and Macmillan who bathed in the warm waters of the 'special relationship' But Heath had also seen that over Suez, or in forcing Macmillan to accept a submarine nuclear deterrent in place of the airborne one which would have been more identifiably a British-controlled and delivered weapon, Washington had regard always to its own interests. Like Britain, America in the early 1970s was going through a wrenching period of change. Nixon was a great foreign affairs strategist but in domestic politics the foreign affairs Dr Jeykll became a Mr Hyde willing to traduce democracy and the American constitution to destroy opponents. In his memoirs Heath blamed Kissinger for failing to understand Europe and thus misleading Nixon. Given that Kissinger had spent time every year since the 1950s travelling to Europe where, fluent in French as well as his own German, he knew European politics and politicians better than most Europeans and almost certainly better than Heath, the charge is absurd. In the Commons, much later, I heard Heath refer to American civilisation, *if you can call it that*. Somewhere he had taken a dislike to Americans – perhaps their culture of Hollywood, Coca-Cola, and rampant market capitalism was unacceptable to a more fastidious, classically-cultured Heath. In a British establishment which was avowedly pro-American, and a Labour Party which had not challenged the United States since Bevin's day, Heath's coolness to the United States was an aberration. What many in Britain disliked about America – its behaviour in Vietnam or the style of its president, Heath admired. What younger British voters admired about America – its open energy, its feminist and civic rights movements, and its youth culture of rock and roll, Heath disliked.

Instead the prime foreign policy focus of Heath's premiership was entry into the EEC. De Gaulle had gone and the new president, Georges Pompidou, was open to British entry, but on French terms. France was unsure where Germany, now under the social democratic leadership of Willy Brandt, was heading. Brandt's *ostpolitik* and seeking new relations with communist states to the east of Germany heralded a new foreign policy confidence in the Federal Republic. German economic strength was growing. From the point of view of Paris, it was better to bring in the great nation state across the Channel to ensure that the EEC would remain *l'Europe des patries* to use de Gaulle's term and not become a federal Europe – a federal Germany writ large. For anti-Europeans it has always been necessary to depict European construction as the end of the nations of Europe and their states. The Labour leader Hugh Gaitskell had set the tone when he said that to enter the EEC would mean Britain would be no more than 'a province of Europe' or, alternatively Britain would be 'no more than a state ... in the United States of Europe, such as Texas and California'. Five decades later this metaphor is still used even though it was nonsense on stilts then and now. The proposition that France (let alone other European states) were, and are, conspiring to give up their own sovereignty and national identity to be controlled by Brussels is a claim the briefest examination would laugh away. As the House of Commons Library has shown, even in 2006 fewer than 10 per cent of all the laws passed in the UK arise from Britain's membership of the European Community, now the EU. The total budget of the EU amounts to just 1 per cent of Europe's gross national income and in monetary terms represents about a quarter of the Pentagon's budget. The key decisions are made or approved by the Council of Ministers. Each person sitting there is elected and accountable to national parliaments and voters. The Commission is dismissed as unaccountable, with unelected bureaucrats, but in 1971 as today, EU commissioners were senior former ministers, acutely aware of domestic politics and the power of national public opinion and conscious that Brussels had to be a self-limiting power-broker in order to succeed. To be sure, there are always those, often at a senior level, who make the case for a greater transfer of powers to Brussels. Margaret Thatcher was the architect of the Single European Market which required a major transfer of sovereignty. In the smaller states of Europe like Luxembourg or Belgium there were always to be found politicians who can produce a plan which contains federal proposals. After all it had been Winston Churchill who had called for 'a kind of United

States of Europe'. But six decades after that speech, it has yet to come about.

Thus Pompidou's warmth towards Heath's bid was not based on extending the power of Brussels over Britain but harnessing the immense strength of British state traditions to help with France to shape a Europe that would work for, not against, the development of the nations and peoples of Europe. Anthony Barber, and when he moved to the Treasury, Geoffrey Rippon, began negotiations for British entry as soon as the new Conservative government was in place. Despite concerns over the growing strength and confidence of the Germans, France was in a stronger position than when Macmillan and Wilson had sought EEC entry. Firstly, the Common Agricultural Policy (CAP), designed to balance to France's advantage the common market in industrial goods which principally benefited German manufacturing strength, was firmly entrenched. Britain would have to accept the CAP and its rules, at the expense of the former white dominions in the Commonwealth. Secondly, France had planted a stake in the heart of supra-nationality with the Luxembourg accord which held that any country could block a community decision if it believed vital national interests were at stake. In shorthand this is known as the national veto. France had swept aside the federalists to make clear EEC development would be at the speed dictated by the nation states.

Heath had little choice but to agree EEC entry terms on conditions acceptable to France. But since the French view of Europe was anti-federal, there was little reason to cavil. Heath sought Willy Brandt's support and the German chancellor said the rest of the six would welcome British entry once French agreement had been secured. Heath had one great asset in his talks with the French. This was the presence of Christopher Soames, the former Tory minister and Churchill's son-in-law, as ambassador in Paris. Outwardly a bluff upper-class Tory, Soames had an acute political brain about European politics and, in contrast to traditional diplomats whose despatches sometimes read like a resumé of the day's press in the capital in which they serve, Soames loved politics and had a cat-like feel for how French politicians worked, supported by his command of the language and affection for the country. In a powerful and prescient analysis sent to London in April 1971, Soames argued that the time had come for Heath to take command of the talks and persuade Pompidou to support UK entry because 'the only people who can unlock the door to us are the French. Whilst they do not enjoy isolation (in the way the General did), the French … believe that in the last resort the Germans will acquiesce in what they decide and the Italians can be fixed. The Belgians they patronise and the Dutch they admire but disregard. So it comes down to an Anglo-French understanding. Finally, until Pompidou had heard himself from the Prime Minister what are the limits beyond which we cannot and will not go, there remains a real risk that he will simply misjudge both how high he can set the hurdle and what a deal with us would really involve for France. If that happened, history would have gone by default.' Soames described Pompidou as 'no European visionary panting for political unification. He is a cautious, hard-bargaining, reticent Auvergnat with limited imagination and no talent for grandeur … The French (from the President down) are waiting for us to make the move – partly for reasons of national pride, but also because nobody here seriously believes that the centuries-old hatchet of Anglo-French animosity can be buried by remote control in Brussels.' Soames urged the tidying up of as many details as possible before the meeting between Heath and Pompidou. 'The French are well aware of our difficulties with public and parliamentary opinion, and the pressure this puts us under to get a quick settlement' but he added that 'gestures of spontaneous good will towards the other party do not exist in the French negotiating repertoire.' What was needed was a new summit so that 'clear political directives are given (and) the French are persuaded that the British are really prepared to put both feet in Europe (as Pompidou puts it).' The British had to move. Although upon entry, Britain would represent more than one-fifth of the total economic output of the EEC, London was proposing that the UK should contribute just 3 per cent to the combined European budget.[9]

In London, Heath was facing a rising tide of hostility to EEC entry. Labour had now come out against it. Douglas Jay had proposed calling a referendum, an idea which Tony Benn had taken up. Jim Callaghan echoed Gaitskell's thousand years of history, when he grandiloquently announced that in the language of Chaucer and Shakespeare his response to the suggestion that Britain should join Europe was "Non, merci beaucoup!' Those like Denis Healey, who had provided the intellectual justification for Ernest Bevin's rejection of the Schuman Plan two decades previously, were hostile.[10] Roy Jenkins refused to turn his coat but with Labour swayed by the new militancy in the trade unions and social movement which saw the EEC as a capitalist plot to impose continental Catholic corporatism on sturdy Protestant parliamentary England, the tide of anti-Europeanism in Labour and unions was rising fast. Tony Crosland, previously pro-European, started to equivocate and joined the anti-European groupings in Labour. Crosland complained that he now had the 'reputation as a trimmer, ditherer, lack of consistency and courage because of Eur[ope] ... [I] won't do much better till Eur[ope] out of the way'.[11] Heath, at least, knew what he believed. Equally honest were Labour former ministers like Peter Shore

Europe

With hindsight it was fitting that the topic of Edward Heath's maiden speech in the House of Commons was Europe. On 26 June 1950 he spoke in favour of the Schuman Plan for a European Coal and Steel Community. Late of the Heavy Anti-Aircraft Regiment, Lieutenant-Colonel Heath had just been visiting Germany, where he had seen an economy already recovering and talked to the new German government and opposition committed to this new vision for European cooperation: *I found that their attitude was governed entirely by political considerations. I believe there is a genuine desire on their part to reach agreement with France and with the other countries of Western Europe. I believe that in that desire the German government are genuine and I believe, too, that the German government would be prepared to make economic sacrifices in order to achieve those political results which they desire. I am convinced that, when the negotiations take place between the countries about the economic details, the German government would be prepared to make sacrifices ... I believe that these discussions would give us a chance of leading Germany into the way we want her to go. It was said long ago in the House that magnanimity in politics is not seldom the truest wisdom. I appeal tonight to the government to follow that dictum, and to go into the Schuman Plan to develop Europe and to coordinate it in the way suggested.* Heath was convinced that here was a chance, *a great chance, perhaps the greatest in twenty years,* to influence the shaping of the future. *By standing aside from any discussions,* Heath predicted, *we may be taking a very great risk with our economy – a very great risk indeed.* 'For Edward Heath, it was an article of faith: and it was rendered the more prominent in his credo, the more vital in his personal history, by the fact that it turned out to be not only his maiden speech but the one speech of any significance he made as a back-bencher in Parliament, before soon being hoisted into the Whips' office and thence, after nine years of managerial silence, to a front-bench position where he spoke from the despatch box.' [Hugo Young, *This Blessed Plot* (Macmillan, London: 1998) p 219.]

and Barbara Castle, who argued against membership of the EEC with unrestrained vigour. Others weasled around by opposing the terms Heath was securing for British entry. The call for a referendum was a comfort blanket for many in Labour who resented being forced to adopt anti-European positions in the name of appeasing rank-and-file militants in constituency parties and shop stewards in the unions.

Heath's chief whip, Francis Pym, warned him that as many as 35 Conservative MPs, led by Enoch Powell, would vote against entry. Thus the parliamentary majority Heath had won in 1970 was far from certain to be sustained the longer negotiations dragged on and the more other domestic troubles in Britain eroded the Prime Minister's authority. Heath had to win Pompidou over and quickly. For two days, 20–21 May 1971, the President and Prime Minister met. The British Embassy in the rue Faubourg St Honoré, taken by Wellington as a spoil of war after Waterloo, is just 200 metres from the Elysée. Both the embassy and the Elysée have beautiful gardens where the two leaders walked and talked. The British Ambassador in Paris has always had one of the best chefs in a country where good food is essential in politics and life. Heath was able to offer Pompidou a dinner based on the solid peasant dishes of his native Auvergne and the signal, in protocol terms, of the French head of state coming to lunch in a foreign country's embassy was important.

These trimmings of a latter-day 'Field of the Cloth of Gold' were important but the heart of the discussion lay in what Heath said to Pompidou. France was far from united in wanting Britain to join the EEC. In an example of reverse Bennism-Powellism, Jean-Marcel Jeanneney, who had served as a minister under both de Gaulle and Pompidou and was a former ambassador, used the pages of *Le Monde*, on the eve of Heath's visit to Paris, to explain why Britain joining the

EEC would be a disaster. As a good Cartesian he advanced three reasons. Firstly, Britain joining the EEC would slowly turn the Common Market into a vast 'free trade zone' with an increasing economic dependence on the United States. Secondly, British diplomats 'using their great skills of divide and rule' would 'inevitably lead to Europe following behind American' foreign policy. The third reason to oppose British entry was cultural. English would become 'the language of politics, science and economic activity'. If for Peter Shore, Enoch Powell and other opponents of the EEC, British entry meant loss of control over Britain's national sovereignty, for Jeanneney the argument was the opposite. Britain joining Europe would mean France 'faced with a major economic crisis would have lost all freedom of action, or during an international conflict [France] would realise she had no freedom of choice and [France] would find her language fading away over time.' For the Gaullist ex-minister these horrors would open the way to Communists finally getting a real audience as spokesmen for French national interests.[12] So if for British opponents of the EEC joining Europe would mean surrendering British sovereignty to wily continentals manipulated by the French, for their opposite numbers in Paris, allowing Britain to join would turn Europe into a satellite of the United States, and, simultaneously allow the Communists to finally achieve their ends. How men of great intellect and profound political gifts can proclaim such self-evident untruths is a matter for the psychoanalyst, not the historian.

The full Foreign Office account of Pompidou's two-day meeting with Heath has only recently been revealed under the Freedom of Information Act. It opened with Pompidou saying 'what was involved was a historic change in the attitude of Britain ... If Britain was really decided to make this change France, in his person, would greatly welcome it.'

Heath played Pompidou skilfully. 'Historically, Britain had always been part of Europe. It was only during the past 25 years that it had come to seem that our natural connection might be with the United States. But we were in fact, still part of Europe; and his government were orientating their policies so as to bring them into line with the European Community.' Heath stroked French sensibilities about the United States. The French writer and politician, Jean-Jacques Servan Schreiber, has recently produced his best-selling *Le défi americain* ('The American Challenge') which painted an apocalyptic picture of the United States, via its multinationals, taking over the world. For Heath, the United States was a problem, not the solution. *There could be no satisfactory partnership, even if Britain wanted it, between two powers one which was barely a quarter the size of the other.* On the contrary Heath's 'purpose was to see a strong Europe, which could speak with a single voice after a full discussion in common of the world problems affecting it, and could then exert effective influence in different parts of the world [and] to exert more effective influence in the field of defence and to contribute more actively to its own security.'[13]

Ever since de Gaulle's rebuff to the first application to join the EEC, Heath had been convinced that an answer lay in solving the discrepancy between France's independent nuclear deterrent and the one that Britain had bought from the Americans. Heath 'suggested in the late 1960s that an Anglo-French strategic nuclear deterrent should be formed and held in trust for the European members of NATO',[14] but Pompidou disabused him. 'Speculation about some kind of Anglo-French nuclear entente was not for the present,' he told Heath at the Elysée.[15] Heath moved on to assure Pompidou that the past history of Britain seeking to divide Europe was over. Pompidou then secured Heath's agreement on the Thatcherist emphasis France placed on the right of national veto. 'If some unacceptable decision affecting vital French interests were taken, France would not allow it to be imposed upon her … If vital interests concerning Britain, Germany or Italy (just as much as France) were at stake, then any decision in the matter must be unanimous.' Heath 'expressed his complete agreement' on this point and said *the people of Britain were concerned at the majority voting provisions in the Treaty of Rome.*

Having removed the nuclear question and agreed that national vetoes would remain at the heart of European construction, Heath and Pompidou then had a long discussion about economy policy and currency discrepancies. For Pompidou, a former banker, who had been one of the architects of the stable and strong franc policy when Prime Minister of France under de Gaulle, the instability of world currencies was of major concern. The United States had broken the fixed rate of the dollar agreed under the Bretton Woods. Europe had sought to respond with a plan put forward by the Prime Minister of Luxembourg, Pierre Werner, to move towards economic and monetary union and a common currency by 1980. But Nixon's aggressive use of the dollar as an instrument of foreign policy was mirrored in Europe by successive devaluations and revaluations in a kind of currency war as European governments sought to offset their failures on the inflation and other domestic economic fronts (soon to be exacerbated by the rise in oil prices) by manipulating currencies.[16] In his talks with Heath, Pompidou was more concerned by the behaviour of the German finance minister, nominally a social democrat, but as Pompidou complained, 'ultra-liberal' on currency matters. Germany had unilaterally floated the Deutschmark to keep inflation down, and allowed the moderate wage increases agreed under the employer-union co-determination system, to sustain the productivity and export performance of German industry.

Heath made the banal point that the government *did not regard sterling as an instrument of prestige nor did they feel sentimental about it; nor did they believe that the future of the City of London as a financial centre depended on the sterling area.* Moreover, the EEC should move to *co-ordinate their monetary policies* at some indeterminate date in the future. In truth, neither Pompidou nor Heath had any concrete policies to propose on the currency problems besetting Europe, or the balance of payments difficulties facing Britain. Clearly, a fully open single market would be difficult to operate if each country within it could alter its prices for exchange of goods and services with its neighbours by devaluing or revaluing its currency. If a pair of Italian shoes can suddenly become 20 per cent cheaper relative to a similar pair of French shoes by fiat of an Italian government devaluing the lire, why should French shoemakers accept this loss of trade? But in 1972 there were still border controls and customs checks in place. The single market led to the euro but this was for the future.

The discussion was technical rather than political. Heath wanted French help to stabilise sterling and avoid the run on the pound that had obliged Wilson to devalue. He was achieving little with his domestic policy aimed at taming inflation and soon would be going in the other direction of relaxing monetary discipline in order to boost growth through higher public spending. In any event, the discussion was irrelevant as the rise in oil prices in 1973 completely threw to the winds any possible monetary convergence between Britain and other European countries, or indeed between France, Germany and Italy.

The highly technical discussions on special drawing rights, the role of the Bank of International Settlement, and other arcane matters of high interest to the former Rothschild employee combined with Heath's solid assurances of Britain being fully committed to a European future worked on Pompidou like a charm. The two men strolled through the garden of the Elysée agreeing with each other. France, of course, was incomparably stronger in relation to Britain than in 1962. The country had regained its confidence. A decade before, de Gaulle was still extricating France from Algeria, and the renewal of French industry, its road system and electricity transmission showed an effective modernising state working hand-in-hand with tough private management promoting a new French capitalism. Britain, by contrast, under Wilson and even in the first year of Heath, seemed gripped by crisis and a lack of leadership on key economic and foreign policy matters. Britain in 1962 was still the victorious Second World War super-power. Britain in 1971 was soon to be dubbed the 'sick man of Europe'. Pompidou could therefore afford to be generous. The United States in 1962 under Kennedy was unquestionably the dominant power in the world, but a decade later, America under Nixon was bogged down in Vietnam, its economy was a mess, its cities and campuses beset by upheavals by the young, by African-Americans, by women and by an American intelligentsia which loathed the federal government. Heath was able to offer the perspective of a Britain detaching herself from America to join Europe. For Pompidou there was a further benefit. The Britain that would join the EEC would weaken forever the federalist dreamers of Brussels and the smaller states whose thinking permeated the Belgian capital. And so it turned out.

Pompidou organised a joint press conference with Heath in the same Salle des Fêtes in the Elysée where de Gaulle had announced his veto in January 1963. Pompidou announced that France would not veto Britain's entry into the EEC. For

Heath, *it was a wildly exciting moment. Just forty years after my first visit to Paris, I had been able to play a part in bringing about the unity of Europe. It was an historic occasion.*[17] Alas, and as so often in Heath's story, the triumph descended into a grumpy, bitter, foot-slog through Parliament and through a country that had not been fully prepared for the historic change Heath had brought about. Pompidou ordered French negotiators to tone down their demands but there was still hard bargaining to be done. Even today, there are criticisms of what was agreed in the talks following the Heath-Pompidou break-through. The question of New Zealand's agricultural imports was dealt with and despite the dire warnings about the threat to the (white) Commonwealth as a result of Heath's agreement, history has shown that Australia, New Zealand and to a different degree Canada were already *en route* to a new and successful way of life. On fishing policy, the Heath government failed to coordinate with the three other applicants for EEC membership – Ireland, Denmark, and Norway – all of which had important coastal fishing interests. Just as Pompidou could not deliver all that a strict interpretation of French national interest might require by way of concession from Britain, so too did Heath's negotiators have to give way.

He returned to an applauding press but the political mood was not so enthusiastic. His chief whip, Francis Pym, told him that there too many Conservative MPs ready to vote no to guarantee a successful passage of the Heath-Pompidou deal through the Commons. Labour was moving towards anti-Europeanism and, as over trade union reform under Wilson, the populist instincts of James Callaghan, led him

Just forty years after my first visit to Paris, I had been able to play a part in bringing about the unity of Europe. It was an historic occasion.

HEATH

to denounce Britain joining an EEC 'determined by a French-Continental European approach'. For Callaghan it was all the fault of the French and their president who 'is no less clear that in so far as British history, our political ideas and our links with the world differ from those of the French-dominated EEC, then Britain must subordinate them to the extent of a complete rupture with our identity'.[18] Callaghan's dishonesty and populist language came back to haunt him as he had to abide by Heath's terms when he became Foreign Secretary in 1974 and then Prime Minister in 1976. Heath's negotiating position was identical to that of the Wilson government, including Callaghan, which had decided to make a fresh application for entry into the EEC in June 1970 had Labour won the election. The EEC commitment was even in the Labour Party manifesto. Never had a governing party stood on its head so fast. Callaghan's opportunist cynicism did lasting damage to a Labour Party which could not make its peace over Europe then and for years afterwards. Many Labour MPs followed the line laid down by the young firebrand MP, Neil Kinnock, who told Labour's special conference in July 1971, 'The opportunity presented to us is the opportunity to lead the British people and kick the Tories out of power ... we cannot with one tongue be the enemies of this class-ridden government and with the other tongue embrace them and follow their policies ... because I am willing to use any weapon to beat them, that I am against EEC entry on these terms at this time'.[19] Kinnock received wild applause for this anti-EEC speech.

'The vital point about Heath, when compared to succeeding three Prime Ministers, was that he was communitaire in his behaviour: no-one could doubt his deep commitment to the Community.'

JOHN YOUNG

Faced with a Labour Party using EEC entry as a stick to beat

Heath, the Prime Minister had to give way to the suggestions that the vote should be a free one. As a former Chief Whip himself he hated the idea of an elected government not being able to get its policies through the Commons, all the more so on an issue which defined his purpose in politics. But the figures were clear. If all parties whipped along existing policy and party lines there would be no majority. The decision to allow a free vote opened the way to a massive majority of 112 for Heath after a tense six-day debate in the Commons. Forty-one Conservatives voted against Europe. Labour pro-Europeans had appealed to Harold Wilson to allow a free vote and the Labour Chief Whip promised pro-Europeans like Bill Rodgers that an anti-European vote would be imposed 'over his dead body.' Wilson caved in to the Callaghan-Kinnock line and 69 Labour MPs had to vote against the party's three-line whip. The young newly-elected Scottish MP John Smith was one of them. Like the even younger Tony Blair, just beginning at Oxford and whose first ever vote was to vote 'Yes' in the 1975 referendum, there was a new Labour generation that saw Britain as a European nation on a par with France and Germany.

Heath had a parliamentary victory to add to his triumph in securing British entry. He went down to Annie's Bar, the little hideaway used only by MPs and lobby correspondents, after the vote was announced and spent two hours enjoying his achievement. The bill to introduce the Treaty of Rome into British law was more closely fought with anti-Europeans like Enoch Powell combining with Michael Foot – the same alliance that had defeated the modernisation of the House of Lords – to make life difficult for Heath. The government was forced to limit debate through guillotine motions to stop anti-EEC filibustering. Pro-European Labour MPs met privately and agreed to be absent on key divisions to balance the anti-

European Tory MPs who were voting with Labour. Equally, Conservative MPs who were hostile to the Common Market did not want to give Labour the pleasure of defeating a Tory government in the division lobbies. Heath had a majority of just eight on the Second Reading and 17 on the Third Reading on 13 July 1972. Britain became a full member of the EEC on New Year's Day, 1973. By then the Heath government had many other problems to deal with. European economies were also beginning to lose some of the shine that had made them so attractive. Britain's economic weakness in the 1970s and 1980s and the impact of oil shocks preventing a modernisation of European economies meant that Britain's financial relationship with the Community continued to be disadvantageous. It was not until the 21st century that Britain and France started to pay roughly the same amount to the overall EU budget. Heath's hopes that Britain in Europe would begin a process of shaping a new world power – a third force – between the United States and the Soviet bloc never came to life. Yet he had made his mark on history. As John Young, the historian of Britain and Europe, wrote: 'The vital point about Heath, when compared to succeeding three Prime Ministers, was that he was *communitaire* in his behaviour: no-one could doubt his deep commitment to the Community; he did not pursue the myth of the special relationship to the detriment of EEC co-operation; and he was popular with other European leaders.'[20] For Heath's biographer, John Campbell, Heath taking Britain into Europe 'may have disappointed in the short run. But it was an historic achievement none the less.'[21]

Chapter 8: Industrial Relations and the Economy, 1970–4

On entering government Heath was committed to two policies developed in opposition, the success of which would eventually suffer from the passage of 'events' in his 44 months in Downing Street. The first was to abolish Labour's income policy and reform the system of collective bargaining and promote individual liberties[1] to counter what the Conservatives perceived to be abuse of power by the unions under the previous Labour rule. They argued that such a move was imperative to enable the government to bring a halt to 'wildly inflationary'[2] wage demands. The Industrial Relations Bill, which had been a Conservative pledge since 1965 and which was immediately introduced in December 1970, aimed to solve these problems. The second policy was to pursue a strategy of non-intervention in failing companies in order to change 'Britain's industrial psychology'. However, the Heath government was forced to U-turn on both of these aspects of long-held policy as a result of a mixture of industrial action, world economic downturn and indecisiveness.

But was there a hand on the rudder? Richard Sennett, in a more recent context, has argued that people distrust, indeed fear, such lack of steady direction on the part of their political leaders. Policy at state level is not a product to be consumed and, once consumed, discarded. In this view

Heath and his ministers may be seen as 'consumers of policy, abandoning them as though they have no value once they· exist. This consuming passion breaks trust in government: the public cannot credit that the policymaker ever believed in the policy he or she once put forward, then left behind.'[3] The public (though this is even more true for a party and for MPs who need to sense organically where they are going) infer 'that politicians are rudderless or lack commitment'.[4] Heath's tacking and going-about on policy left his party and the nation unclear as to where he wanted to take them. His store of trust, which was high in 1970, slowly ebbed away.

The difficulties faced in making the Industrial Relations Bill work presented an early setback for the Heath government. Heath did not anticipate the opposition the Bill would receive from the trade unions, mainly because of the mandate he felt the government had from the public, but also because trade union leaders had led him to believe in opposition that they would support it. Heath had invited trade union leaders like Vic Feather, the TUC general secretary, and Jack Jones, leader of the biggest trade union, the Transport and General Workers' Union to dinner at his flat in the Albany. He played the Labour Party anthem, the Red Flag, on the piano and Jones noted 'There is no doubting Ted Heath's sympathy for people and we quickly established a feeling of camaraderie.'[5] The comrades in the unions had other views. Militant trade unionism had been encouraged by the defeat of the *In Place of Strife* proposals put forward in 1969 by Harold Wilson's Employment Secretary, Barbara Castle which in Robert Taylor's judgement 'soured relations inside the Labour Movement and made a contribution to the eventual defeat of the Labour Party at the June 1970 general election'.[6] As soon as Heath was elected he was faced with a damaging dock strike. The whole period of Heath's three and a half years in office was dominated by strikes in different industries. Had Heath sought to modernise British industrial relations with a radical reform of the labour market players, he might have looked to his beloved Europe for a Continental model. There the closed shop was unknown and in most countries a system of labour courts adjudicated disputes which in Britain were 'solved' by face-to-face confrontation between managers and shop stewards or union officials. In many countries, a legal minimum wage meant that wage exploitation of the lowest-paid was avoided. In some countries, employees had seats on the board of companies thus binding them in more closely to top managers. In Germany, union rules required a vote in a secret ballot of three-quarters of all union members before a strike could be launched. Wage negotiations were tough but based on a union analysis of what the economy could sustain as a whole and where inflation would be in the future. In Nordic countries and Germany, all workers in an industry belonged to the same union. No British union, however, wanted to modernise along Continental lines.

Wage increases outstripped productivity in dramatic fashion. In May 1969, pay settlements averaged 4.6 per cent, but by July 1970 average wages were increasing by 15.2 per cent, twice the rate of price increases while underlying productivity was going up by a miserable 3 per cent. The UK's average annual growth between 1960 and 1970 had been just 2.8 per cent, half that of France and Germany, or of Western Europe as a whole where growth had average 5.8 per cent each year in the decade preceding Heath becoming Prime Minister. Labour's response to wage inflation out-stripping prices and productivity had been to bring in a statutory incomes policy which the more free-market Heath wanted to avoid. The other alternative advocated by the Right was a reversion to classic 1930 monetarism and to use mass unemployment as a means of breaking union power and controlling inflation, but Heath had no time for that ideology. Moreover, the Conservative Party also did not see unions as 'the enemy within', to use Margaret Thatcher's later phase. Union refusal to reform, the posturing of leaders, and rank and file militancy helped destroy three successive governments – Wilson in 1970, Heath in 1974 and Callaghan after the 'Winter of Discontent' strikes of 1979. Iain Macleod, the cleverest of Heath's Shadow Cabinet, had been Labour Minister in the last Tory government and argued in 1963 against legislation on industrial relations as it 'would lose us the backing of the trade unions upon which our victory at a General Election ultimately depended'. Macleod continued, 'legislation would cut across the present policy of trying to bring about a general improvement in industrial relations on a voluntary basis ... it would end the prospect of further progress [and] cause a head-on collision with the trade union movement.'[7] Macleod was dead by the time the new government came to put forward its proposals in 1970. For Heath, if incomes policy and mass unemployment were to be avoided the logic led to trying to reform the unions and make them a support mechanism for a modern economy rather than the opposite.

The government proposals were based largely on the ideas Heath had developed in opposition and included in the 1966 election manifesto. The main proposal was to revoke the immunities that unions enjoyed under law and lay them open to being sued or prosecuted if they failed to abide by the legally enforceable collective agreements. In addition, a new body, the Official Registrar, would have the right to supervise union rulebooks. The Bill, which became the Industrial Relations Act in 1971, unleashed a storm of union anger not seen since the politicised industrial action and demonstrations of the early 1920s. The Labour Party swung behind the unions, sensing an opportunity to hit the government. The new Employment Secretary, Robert Carr, presented the government's proposals as a take-it-or-leave-it package. In opposition he had wanted a more piecemeal policy, tackling each issue of concern separately – the policy later adopted by the Conservatives after 1979 – and making sure new rules were in place before advancing to fresh legislation. Instead, the Industrial Relations Bill was a clumsy leviathan of a law with too many proposals which the trade unions could simply run rings around. Heath opened the debate on the second day of the Bill's passage through the Commons in December 1970. Tying his authority as Prime Minister to the Bill was an error as it further increased a militant rejectionism by trade unions, the Labour Party, and the energetic *soi-disant* marxists now active in many trade unions.

The main aim of the Bill was to reduce the number of unofficial strikes by making the results of collective bargaining legally binding unless both parties agreed otherwise. The government failed to predict that this loophole would be exploited by the unions who only needed to rubber-stamp an agreement with the words 'This Is Not a Legally Enforceable Agreement' to get around the legislation. Alongside this was a new code of industrial practice which if broken would remove legal immunity. The National Industrial Relations Court (NIRC) would be set up as a new branch of the High Court to enforce the code and trade unions would be expected to register with it. The Bill also included measures which would allow a 60-day 'cooling-off' period and a requirement to hold a secret ballot before strike action. The right to belong or *not* belong to a trade union was also introduced – the first time it had been on the statute book. This threatened the closed shop system which had been the bulwark of shop steward and workplace union power in many industries.

In his speech during the passage of the Bill, Heath blithely said *I do not believe for one moment that the unions are likely to put themselves in breach of the law* – an underestimation for sure. The passage of the Bill was not helped by the fact that the government had to simultaneously negotiate with the unions over pay. Heath felt that it was the government's duty to 'lead by example' by keeping down wage demands from those employed in the public sector. Heath put an early toe into the tricky waters of incomes policy by putting forward a principle that pay deals should be slightly lower than the previous one, in a hope that inflation would then start to reverse. This policy became known as the 'n-i' policy. This was immediately ignored in the first main pay dispute in November 1970 by local authority dustmen and sewage workers who were given a 14 per cent increase, very close to what they had demanded. This meant that the government had to redouble its efforts to control wages over those it could more easily influence, including the nationalised industries. Their first test was on 7 December when power workers decided to work to rule hoping to gain a pay increase of 25 per cent. In the cold of winter this had a particularly harsh effect on the general public and there was a run on candles. The government responded by putting a State of Emergency in place and appointing Lord Wilberforce to negotiate the claim while considering 'the public interest'. The final settlement in February 1971 was claimed by Heath to be 'one of our few strokes of good fortune during this period', but others were less positive claiming that the award of around

> *I do not believe for one moment that the unions are likely to put themselves in breach of the law.*
>
> HEATH

15–19 per cent broke the norm of 'n-i' and set a dangerous precedent.

The passage of the Industrial Relations Bill, meanwhile, was becoming more fraught. The Committee Stage of the Bill was taken on the floor of the House of Commons contributing to over 100 hours of parliamentary time, the longest for any Bill since 1945 except those dealing with finance. Despite the amount of time dedicated to the Bill, the guillotine prevented any discussion of the new NIRC which perhaps contributed to the difficulties encountered later in its set-up. The more damaging opposition, however, was not faced in the chamber, but in the 'day of protest' organised by the TUC which saw over 120,000 union members holding aloft placards asking to 'Kill The Bill'. It was during this period that the unions decided on a plan which would eventually scupper the legislation – a tactic of simply refusing to register with the NIRC. By the time the Act came into force in 1972, 146 unions had deregistered under the terms of the Act even though this also prevented them from realising the other benefits and immunities under the Act. In effect, the Act was dead. Attempts to arrest dockers who had organised an unofficial – under the Act, an illegal – strike ended in farce as scores of thousands of workers stopped work to protest and the government had to find an hitherto unknown legal officer, called the Official Solicitor, to release the men from jail.

The other main plank of Heath's economic policy was to stop propping up ailing industries – so-called 'lame ducks', a phrase used by the Trade and Industry Secretary John Davies. This turned out to be a hostage to fortune as the phrase was turned against the government when they were later forced to backtrack on the non-interventionist sentiment. In his autobiography Heath maintained that their purpose was more pragmatic than simply being non-interventionist and that they never had a policy of total non-intervention, but the hardliners in his party were happy to leap on future help to failing industries as a u-turn. The main instance of this was in relation to the dire financial situation of Rolls-Royce which had secured a contract to supply a new engine for an aircraft manufactured by Lockheed. The company had seriously underestimated the costs of the project and was asking the government to help bail them out.

At first glance this seemed to be exactly the right situation for the government to prove their principles – it was after all a contract negotiated by a private company and their fault for messing up the cost analysis. There were a number of factors, however, which meant that the government could not realistically turn away from the problem. There were concerns that failure to support Rolls-Royce could lose defence capability for the UK, discourage investment in 'high-technology' which the government had said they were committed to, potentially cost 40,000 direct and indirect jobs, ruin relations with the Americans, and have a bad knock-on effect for the City. All this taken together convinced the Cabinet that the government should contribute around 70 per cent of the shortfall. This turned out not to be enough however, and the decision was taken to nationalise the company, though it retained the structure of a private company, and was eventually re-privatised in 1987. Heath's view was that to have done otherwise would have made them *guilty of letting down our country*, and even hardliners such as Norman Tebbit acknowledged that this was a special case.

Similar concessions were made in the case of Mersey Docks which was in trouble because of bad management decisions and fees which had been kept low in expectation of nationalisation. The Cabinet decided to keep funding the docks on the condition that the company was reorganised under a new chairman. One of the main considerations was the loss of jobs in Merseyside which already had its unemployment problems, but it seemed to some people that Heath's rhetoric about non-intervention did not match the reality. On the other hand, however, the government did end support for the Upper Clyde Shipbuilders, and stood firm in the face of a 'work-in'. There were also a few cases of privatisation to uphold Heath's position, including selling off the travel agents Thomas Cook and Lunn Poly, as well as a state-run brewery, and forcing the state airlines to relinquish some routes to independent providers. Compared to the amount of state money used to save Rolls-Royce, however, these seemed like relatively small gestures towards privatisation.

Wage inflation and unemployment meanwhile continued to rise in 1971, and the growth figures of 3 per cent projected by the Treasury looked rather optimistic. The response of the Chancellor Tony Barber in his Budget of March 1971 was to concentrate on giving people incentives to save and businesses incentives to invest. He cut corporation tax by 2.5 per cent, halved selective employment tax and announced a new Value Added Tax to start in 1973. Barber also increased tax allowances for children. By July, however, this did not seem to have had any effect so Barber introduced further measures including an 18 per cent cut in purchase tax, and measures to give business incentives to invest in machinery. Alongside these reforms, a programme of investment in roads, railways and housing was announced in specific regional areas to help spur development.

At the end of his first 18 months in office, Heath was not seen as the failure later right-wing Tories would describe him as. Writing on 31 December 1971, Tony Benn saw the Prime Minister thus: 'However much one may dislike Heath – and I personally find him a very unattractive person – he had emerged as a strong and tough Prime Minister who is prepared to face battles and fight them out. The economy, after having gone through a difficult eighteen months, is going to pick up and will look good and although unemployment won't drop to acceptable levels and prices won't be held in check, the position won't be too bad from Heath's point of view. He has settled the Rhodesian question by selling out to Smith. He has got us into Europe by accepting conditions that maybe are not ideal. He has emerged as a competent man who can deal with America – so he would claim – meeting Nixon in Bermuda and ending the special relationship. These are things which represent an historic trend, and I think after Wilson, who appeared as rather a trickster, the public quite like the feeling of Heath as the strong man Prime Minister under whom Britain can hold up her head again.'[8] Benn's interesting and generous assessment is worth quoting at length as later historiography of the Heath government has tended to present it as one disaster limping to another. Heath was the penultimate Prime Minister to try and seek to govern by consensus. The quarter-century since the arrival in office of Margaret Thatcher and Ronald Reagan has seen the rise of a right-wing orthodoxy which obliged centre-left politicians like Bill Clinton and Tony Blair to adapt to doctrines of inequality and *laissez-faire* capitalism that a Roosevelt or an Attlee rejected. But few political leaders can escape the mood of the time if they wish to win power and hold power which has to be based on the centre of the ideological axis at any given time. Ronald Butt, writing in 1974, claimed that 'In the past decade, the whole vocabulary of political and social debate has been captured by the Left, whose ideology has fundamentally remained unanswered by the Conservatives. Where the Conservative Party has answered back, it has done so by conceding half the case that it should have been rebutting and has utterly sought to appease the "trend"'.[9]

Heath therefore must be located in a continuum of British post-war political history. Had he come to be Prime Minister later he might have taken harder, harsher decisions and agreed that the unemployment and terrible regional poverty associated with the 1980s and early 1990s was a price worth paying. Each democracy gets the labour movement actors it deserves. Heath's misfortune was to inherit a trade union movement radicalised by the Wilson years, a management system utterly unable to improve productivity to match continental levels, and a new political excitement in the Labour Party and other political groups who, infused with what might be called the spirit of 1968, dreamt of permanent revolution rather than the duller world of permanent reformism which was and is the only way forward for successful democratic politics. British employers as a class were also indifferent to reforming their approach to labour relations and many looked to a tough Tory government to curtail and corral the unions. For tripartite (government-employer-union) relations to work both employers and unions have to be intelligent. Heath did not enjoy clever social partners in his period of power.

Despite continuing troubles with inflation, as 1972 opened, Heath was still opposed to the option of introducing statutory controls on wage inflation. Instead he pursued a voluntary approach in the hope that the unions and the Confederation of British Industry (CBI) would reach a satisfactory agreement on their own. That this position was unsustainable became more obvious to Heath after the start of troubles with the miners in July 1971. In November they started an overtime ban because the National Coal Board only offered them an 8 per cent increase instead of the 45 per cent they demanded. On 9 January 1972 a national strike was called for the first time in 50 years, heralding a new epoch in working class militancy as flying pickets were sent by Arthur Scargill, the militant head of the National Union of Mineworkers (NUM) in Yorkshire, to try to cut coal supplies to power stations. The Chief Constable of Birmingham, a buffoonish figure more interested in the fortunes of rugby than maintaining law and order, failed to send enough police officers to keep open an important coal depot at Birmingham. I witnessed events there partly as a young BBC radio reporter and partly as a sympathiser for the plight of the miners whose wages did not seem to my and many eyes to match the difficulties of their job and the injuries and deaths they suffered as they dug the coal to power Britain. This coincided with unemployment reaching one million for the first time since 1947. Labour MPs caused such a storm in the Commons the Speaker was forced to suspend the sitting. Moreover the Cabinet was also struggling with bombings in Northern Ireland and negotiations over enabling legislation for entry into the EEC. Any Cabinet would have felt seriously embattled during the early months of 1972.

Lord Wilberforce was asked to conduct an independent enquiry into miners' wages and put forward a deal that was more than the government wanted, but there was still opposition from the NUM. Heath would not give in to any more and eventually at 2.30 a.m. the President, Joe Gormley, backed down on the additional pay increases in return for other fringe benefits. This was still a huge defeat for Heath, as he acknowledged in a broadcast on 27 February 1972 in which he said that *everyone has lost ... in the kind of country we live in there cannot be any 'we' or 'they' ... . there*

In the kind of country we live in there cannot be any 'we' or 'they' ... . there is only us – all of us.

HEATH

is only us – all of us. Combined with civil unrest and the knock-on effect on production of the miner's strikes, finding a way forward for a pay policy became more urgent and was suggested by Vic Feather, General Secretary of the TUC, as the best way forward. In March 1972 therefore, Heath invited the TUC General Council and the CBI to discuss how such situations could be handled in the future. If for militants at union conferences, the rhetoric of class war was reaching new heights, for union leaders, Heath was a man they could do business with. Jack Jones was invited down to Chequers and talks with Heath 'strengthened my conviction that he genuinely wanted to get on with working people'. But Jones and other union leaders who met Heath wanted him to repeal the Industrial Relations Act as well as make massive concessions on prices, pensions, council house rents (which had become politicised after a new Housing Act) which turned local government into an arena of intraparty fighting. Councillors from Clay Cross, a mining village in Derbyshire, refused to implement the Housing Act and ended up in prison, thus further inflaming Labour movement politics. Jones records that 'To the surprise of the trade union side, Ted Heath declared that certain important items we had been emphasising – pensions, rents, the impact of EEC membership, the Industrial Relations Act – were outside the scope of negotiation. Such matters, we were told, were for the House of Commons to determine. A rigid posture was suddenly adopted by the government; even to this day I am unable to understand why.'[10] Others might ask why a handful of trade union leaders assumed they should tell a democratically elected government what its policies and legislation should be in areas well beyond the negotiating and representing role of unions in the workplace. On the other hand, the trade unions had made the Industrial Relations

Act irrelevant by refusing to register under its provision. The Director General of the CBI, Campbell Adamson, stated that the Act had 'sullied every relationship at national level between unions and employers' and as Andrew Taylor has written, 'By the summer of 1972 the Act was effectively dead but continued to poison relations with the government.'[11]

Tripartite meetings were held throughout 1972 to reach a settlement on wage increases and price rises, but despite many hours of banging heads together the unions failed to reach agreement with the government and CBI. This led to a unilateral decision by the government to press ahead with a non-voluntary route, and that it would start with a freeze on prices, wages, rents and dividends for 90 days. Heath made clear that he was unhappy about having had to take such action, but it was broadly welcomed with many people suggesting it ought to have taken place earlier. It is obvious, however, that this was a significant U-turn compared to the manifesto commitments, and despite Heath's contention that it did not represent *a departure from our underlying aims and objectives*, it is hard to see how that fits with the Conservatives original objectives of getting the state out of negotiations on wages.

On the economic front, despite the incentives introduced in Barber's 1971 budgets investment in manufacturing had actually fallen. This led the 1972 Budget to concentrate on a more dramatic measure of extending capital grants to 100 per cent for the first year of industrial investment across the whole country. The subsequent 'Industry Act' was called by some to be a 'socialist' measure, but Heath's response in his autobiography maintains it was *a sensible, pragmatic and practical response to a disappointing state of affairs*. Most of this investment, however, was undermined by the oil crisis which was precipitated by Egypt's attack on Israel on 6 October

1973. Despite keeping up good relations with Arab producers the price of oil rose from $2.40 a barrel at the beginning of 1973 to more than $5 by October. After an OPEC meeting in late December oil increased further to over $11 a barrel. To add to the problems, the NUM put in a pay claim which asked for increases of up to 50 per cent for some workers and saw an opportunity to use the oil crisis to get a better bargaining position. Mick McGahey, a Communist member of the NUM executive, made no bones about the fact that this was an attempt to bring down the government. In his autobiography Heath called it *the unacceptable face of trade unionism*. After having introduced a three-day week Heath in the end felt he had no other option except to request a dissolution of Parliament on 6 February 1974. The NUM had already announced that they planned a new strike to begin that day. In the end the calling of the election was too late to save Heath's government – Mick McGahey and the other militants won the day.

Heath had first met Jack Jones during the Spanish Civil War. He never gave up the belief that Britain's working people had right on their side as they sought through their unions to achieve a fairer world in the workplace. Heath remained firmly in the corporatist-consensual tradition of the 1945 settlement. It is unfair and ahistorical to ask him to be ahead of his time. Later apostles of post-Heath Toryism like Keith Joseph, Nicholas Ridley and above all Margaret Thatcher raised no challenges to the way Heath sought to navigate between the Scylla of wage-hike inflation and the Charybdis of employer-union agencies unable to reform or re-invent themselves. David Marquand has argued that successful European economic and labour market models (successful at the time of his writing his book, *The Unprincipled Society*, two decades ago) were influenced 'by solidaristic social-democratic and social-Christian political philosophies and therefore offered fertile soil to the solidaristic neo-corporatist values of power-sharing and class collaboration'.[12] For the political philosopher Marquand, himself a Labour MP during the Heath government, the Britain of that era simply did not have a political culture of power-sharing based on 'a readiness to accept the responsibilities of power; class collaboration demands a sense of class solidarity; neither is possible unless those concerned are prepared to subordinate short-term self interest to a wider long-term interest. All of this is as foreign to the values of British trade unions and employers' associations as to the structures.'[13] Lamenting the failure of one's country to be modelled on other nations' or regions' systems is sport for political scientists and commentators. Heath was trying to create a United Kingdom that corresponded to his own vision of sensible, rational, law-based labour-market agreements, but he did not create the culture that might have allowed this to happen. Starting off with tough free-market, non-interventionist declarations he quickly reverted to incomes policy, subsidies for weak industries and massive public expenditure boosts. He did not understand the new culture of resistance in unions and a new working class which was less willing to march obediently behind union leaders. His reforms were neither radical enough to create new patterns of support and energy to get them through, nor gradual enough to allow by political osmosis a change in behaviour that would bring about desired results without the *Stürm und Drang* of one of Wagner's operas Heath enjoyed.

In his autobiography, Jack Jones maintains that if Heath has referred the miners' dispute that shut down electricity in homes and hospitals in the miserably cold weather of January and February 1974 to some of kind of independent commission then a solution could have been found without the need for an election. It is true that in modern democracies, asking voters the question 'Who governs?' often brings the response 'Not you'. The French President, Jacques Chirac, called early national assembly elections in 1997, as a reaction against strikes and streets protests opposed to his government's efforts at labour market and welfare reforms. The response of the French voters in 1997 was to elect a socialist government just as the response of British voters in 1974 was to elect a Labour government. That the Wilson-Callaghan administration, 1974–9, could find no answers to the problems Heath also failed to solve was of little consolation. Perhaps there are just moments in history when a nation has to find its own way to a different tomorrow because its political leaders cannot find a way to break free from yesterday's orthodoxies. Heath's defeat in 1974 brought to an end 30 years of seeking to manage Britain without reforming or modernising Whitehall, politics, business or unions. Heath paid the price of loss of office. Reforming a nation to meet the challenges of modernity in any era requires leadership that no-one of that era was able to offer.

Chapter 9: Ulster and Reform of Government

In his magisterial biography of Edward Heath published in 1993, John Campbell avers that 'Few today seriously expect to find a "solution"' to the problem of Ulster.[1] Two decades before this was not how it was seen. Heath's decision to suspend Stormont – the Ulster parliament where the Protestant supremacists held sway – was considered by Andrew Roth to be a move offering 'a small glimmer at the end of the Irish tunnel', 'which was applauded by Labour for doing what the Wilson government contemplated but had not quite dared to do'.[2] Both biographers of Heath were wrong. The troubles in Ulster continued apace for nearly 25 years after direct rule was imposed and yet when a Prime Minister arrived who was able to broker peace, Tony Blair found himself using policies that Heath had initiated.

The decision to split the 19th-century Liberal Party on the question of Ireland when a group of Liberal MPs moved across to join the Conservatives in opposition to Home Rule for Ireland had been the last building block in the Conservative coalition that was the dominant political force in Britain in the 20th century. The Tory Prime Minister at the beginning of the century, Lord Salisbury, declared that he would no more give the vote to an Irishman than to a 'hottentot'. The contempt for Irish identity ran deep in the Tory party. The

111

war of Irish independence had given rise to a British statelet in the north-east of the island with a parliament, Stormont, and officials who had pompous titles like Prime Minister. Catholic workers and citizens suffered discrimination which led in the late 1960s to civil rights marches and demonstrations which were brutally repressed by Protestant militias. Harold Wilson once observed with astonishment Sir Alex Douglas-Home hastily switching his old Etonian tie for a unionist tie with the Red Hand of Ulster on it before a broadcast to the province. For Wilson and most mainland politicians, Northern Ireland was a far-away region of which they knew nothing.

That ignorance came to a dramatic end when Protestant police and militia ran amok in Catholic ghettoes. For the dormant Irish Republican Army (IRA), in its different ideological manifestations, it was a rebirth and validation of violence against the British. The Irish constitution was irredentist and claimed the six counties as part of Ireland. The Labour government decided to send regular British Army units to try and keep the peace but James Callaghan, the Home Secretary, who dealt with the matter did little to meet the demands of the Catholic population for equality of access to jobs and a fair system of political representation.

At first the British soldiers were welcomed as peacemakers but as political reform failed to follow their arrival, the gunmen took over. Had Gerry Adams and other ultra-nationalists chosen to follow the slogan of their youth and make love not war, the Catholic population of Ulster would soon have become big enough to out-vote the more restrained procreation patterns of the Protestants. The violence reached frightening heights very quickly: 13 soldiers and civilians had been killed in 1969, but the death toll was 174 in 1971 (the year when the first British soldier was killed by the IRA),

467 in 1972, and 250 in 1973. Heath had described the *bitter, tribal loathing between the hardline elements in the two communities, springing for an atavism which most of Europe discarded long ago*.[3] (Not true in the Basque country, Corsica, or much of the Western Balkans. Ulster alas showed not the exceptionalism of the island region of Europe but how easy it can be for the civilised veneer of Europe to tear apart to reveal blind, murderous hatreds.) Reginald Maudling, the Home Secretary, made a visit to Northern Ireland and came back with the comment, 'God, what a bloody awful place!'

'God, what a bloody awful place!'
REGINALD MAUDLING ON ULSTER

Lamenting or condemning the hatreds within and between the Protestant Unionist and Catholic Nationalist communities did not constitute a policy. When Heath did move he made a strategic blunder that was to create far worse problems than it solved and provide a massive boost to the hard-liners on both sides. Heath decided to seek to intern without due process those whom the army and Protestant-controlled security forces deemed to be responsible for violence. The internment was a disaster. Like a throwback to the 1930s or events in some British colony, the world watched with consternation as camps were opened to take the sleepy, bewildered, often quite elderly men who were rounded up on 1 August 1971 and interned. Some were terrorist organisers. Most, if not all, active IRA leaders and gunmen slipped across the border to Ireland. The lists provided by the provinces' intelligence services were badly out-of-date. Many of the men interned were subject to degrading treatment which was in breach of the European Convention on Human Rights (ECHR), as was internment without trial itself. Britain had drafted the ECHR and it was supervised by the Council of Europe which Churchill had helped set up after 1945, so Heath the

European had to face the criticisms and condemnation of his policy from the very European institutions he believed in so strongly.

Heath tried to make amends by inviting the Irish prime minister to talks in London and Chequers and made the Unionist prime minister join the talks. This was an important breach in the firmly-held Unionist view that anything to do with Ulster was only a matter for United Kingdom politicians. Inviting Jack Lynch, the Irish government chief, to help find a solution was an important initiative. But just when politics might have taken hold, the military-security community which has its own logic compounded the blunder over internment. On Sunday 30 January 1972, paratroopers opened fire on a civil rights march in Derry, shooting a number of unarmed demonstrators in the back. It was like a scene from South America or Asia with soldiers mowing down unarmed political demonstrators. That the IRA was present and that its leaders cynically used the civil rights movement as a shield for their own terrorism was not in question. But the killings produced explosions of anger in Ireland as the British Embassy was burnt down in Dublin. Heath headed a government that could not maintain peace, let alone democratic law and order in a corner of Europe. The army did eventually restore some kind of order after a massive military operation to re-occupy parts of Derry and Belfast under control of the IRA. Units were flown in from Germany to be used in one of the biggest military operations against an 'enemy' ever seen on British soil. Recently declassified Defence Ministry files reveal that the warship HMS *Fearless*, equipped with helicopters and capable of launching Harrier aircraft, was used to land giant armoured bulldozers in the middle of the night in Northern Ireland which smashed their way through republican barricades.[4] The navy then waited 'over the horizon' as back-up.[5] This was not known at the time but indicates the depth of despair in Downing Street that the Royal Navy should be made ready to take action against part of the United Kingdom.

Heath's political response was to suspend Stormont, remove the affable but bumbling Reginald Maudling as the minister in charge of Northern Ireland and instead send his most trusted lieutenant, William Whitelaw, to impose direct rule on the province with a new Cabinet department set up to administer the province. Maudling meanwhile had had to resign because of what later would be known as 'sleaze', as police were investigating his business links with a building contractor who had bribed his way to win local government contracts. Taken with the departure from government of Lord Jellicoe, Heath's leader of the House of Lords who abruptly resigned after his name was linked with visits to prostitutes, the Heath administration was the first post-war government in which the personal behaviour of senior cabinet ministers, rather than their political or policy failures, became matters of public and publicity interest and caused damage to the overall standing of the administration.

Heath's imposition of direct rule brought little peace. The IRA now had a direct target, the British government, and their ultra-nationalism demanding a withdrawal from all of Ireland was impossible to meet as the long-established Protestant community in the north had no intention of giving up their Britishness. But suspending Stormont did force other political forces in the province to reconsider their positions. Heath brought them all to Sunningdale in December 1973 together the Irish and British governments, to hammer out the power-sharing Sunningdale Agreement with its path-breaking proposal to create a Council of Ireland which would give Dublin *un droit de regard* on the six counties. The

Sunningdale Agreement however provoked an extremist Protestant backlash. With Gerry Adams and Sinn Fein/IRA at one end of the spectrum and Ian Paisley and the various 'volunteer' Protestant death squads and militias at the other end, the space for a constitutional, democratic, rule-of-law politics was limited. The failure of the Sunningdale process belongs to a later government. Seeking a solution to the imbroglio of Northern Ireland was to elude Heath's immediate successors.

For 50 years since Lloyd George and Churchill had bought peace at the price of dividing the island and leaving the Catholics of the north without rights or politics, Ulster had been waiting to explode back into history. It was Heath's tragedy that it happened on his watch. He made things worse with blunders like internment and a failure to control trigger-happy paratroopers. But he was also brave in removing Stormont and bringing Dublin firmly into a new relationship with London which acknowledged finally, if to the fury of the Unionist fanatics, that Ireland was a sovereign nation with a right to have its say on what happened on the common soil of the Irish island. That Heath did not solve the problem and that he let loose the bogey of Ulster politics linking up with right-wing Tories like Enoch Powell was not his fault. But Ulster added to the list of problems that Heath could not find solutions for. His intentions were good but his execution and long-term strategic thinking did not match his ambitions or the nation's needs. On Ulster as on many other issues, Heath was a Prime Minister who was a prisoner, not a master of events.

Heath's government ushered in the biggest transformation of local government since the 19th century. His approach to governance was set out in his speech to the first Conservative Party conference of his government. Heath announced his desire to reorganise Whitehall and review the functions of government – an aspiration which had its nucleus in his time as a civil servant from 1946–7. He expressed the ambition to embark on *a revolution so quiet and yet so total, that it will go... far beyond this decade and way into the 1980s.*[6] The 'quiet revolution' speech was widely applauded as being a bold enunciation of the way Heath intended government to change under his leadership. Unfortunately from Heath's point of view, the turn of events throughout Heath's four years was not to reward his efforts to continue, on his terms, the consensus-corporatist policies in industrial relations and incomes policy after the failure of the Industrial Relations Act. However, one area which benefited from his foresight was institutional reform within the government machine. John Campbell in his biography of Heath called it 'the most ambitious attempt to reshape the structure of government since 1918'.[7]

The first major changes to government were introduced in a White Paper in October 1970 which created two 'super-ministries': the Department of Trade and Industry (DTI) (which is still in existence) and the Department of the Environment. The reason for the restructuring was to ensure that conflicts were resolved in departments rather than bringing problems to Cabinet. Heath also wanted to create a DTI that was large enough to challenge the Treasury, reflecting perhaps his own experience at the Board of Trade in 1963–4. Under the lead of John Davies the DTI never really gained this status, but once Peter Walker was given the helm in 1972 the Treasury's influence did subside, though possibly because Heath was fed up with their advice by that time. The main problem, however, was that the departments were in the end too large, resulting in future Prime Ministers splitting them up again.

The next stage of reform was to introduce a system of

Heath at Number 10

'No Prime Minister since Lloyd George in 1916–17 had made such a deliberate and determined attempt to remodel the whole machinery of state. Like Lloyd George, Heath saw such matters as first-order problems to be tackled as a priority and not as optional extras. They were integral to what he saw as a more focused form of Cabinet government – the traditional collective approach but a sharpened version – another example, perhaps, of the "better yesterday" impulse (though Lloyd George"s brand was much more a tilt towards Prime Ministerial government than was Heath"s: Keynes was right to fear for the Constitution under LG). Both LG and Heath saw change as a symbiosis of improving process and outcome, or management and policymaking. Mrs Thatcher, a more Lloyd Georgian premier than Heath, concentrated almost solely on management reforms. Conviction politicians tend not to be overly fascinated by the quality of policy analysis.

Heath"s memoirs, *The Course of My Life*, are eloquent on the "firm conviction" with which he entered No. 10 "that we needed to change the structure of government ... a subject which engrossed me ... because I was concerned that Ministers spent too much time on day-to-day matters, instead of on strategic thinking." At his first Tuesday evening audience with the Queen he placed "at the top of the list, the formation of the government, civil service matters and the place of businessmen in the work of government... ."

Once in office, Heath told a pair of *Evening Standard* journalists how he found machinery of government questions "of extraordinary interest" and railed against the lack of strategic focus of the Cabinets in which he had sat as Chief Whip or as a minister under Eden, Macmillan and Douglas-Home: "I had seen Cabinets which all the time seemed to be dealing with the day-to-day problems and there was never a real opportunity to deal with strategy, either from the point of view of the Government or the country. What I wanted to do was to change things that the Cabinet could do that.'"[Hennessy, *The Prime Minister*, pp 337–8.]

'Programme Analysis and Review' (PAR) which was heavily influenced by US business practice. The purpose of PAR was to cut bureaucracy and waste – both to free up resources, but also to fulfil a key goal of getting government out of those areas which Heath thought should rightly be dealt with by society. In more modern terminology, PAR sought to get value for money for taxpayers. Heath was aware that once departments were given money for specific circumstances *they seldom reappraised the machinery and money* and everything was just allowed *to rumble on*.[8] As with all attempts to reform government, however, PAR's success, or lack of it, was a result of Civil Service hostility. The Treasury in particular was highly suspicious of the changes and as a result very few savings were actually found. This was compounded by the fact that no-one could find any other substantial government roles to get rid of except for ones already earmarked before the election.

It was events, however, which really shelved PAR. Once the government was faced with increasing unemployment and economic crisis in 1973 they responded with a 'dash for growth' which resulted in an increase of around 400,000 civil servants rather than a decrease which was the original objective. During this time PAR became counter-productive and turned into a shackle on departments. It was eventually abolished by Mrs Thatcher, but it did however contribute to the thinking behind the 'Efficiency Unit' and 'Next Steps'– two programmes deliberately set up to bring more private sector experience into the Whitehall operation. Another short-lived change in approach at the beginning of Heath's government was the importing of businessmen such as Derek Rayner into Whitehall mainly because of a lack of support from within the civil service bureaucracy. It was Thatcher again who adopted this idea, and Rayner was in fact brought back into government in 1979. Heath's desire to turn government into management and his fondness for importing business leaders was lampooned by *Private Eye* as turning Britain into 'Heathco' – a business outfit headed by Heath. Mockery apart, Heath did realise that the 19th century Civil Service, so proud of itself, needed modernising. It still does and always will.

The best-known Heath innovation was the creation of the Central Policy Review Staff (CPRS). This body was charged with 'thinking the unthinkable' and providing a running critique of whether the government was achieving its ambitions. Douglas Hurd in his memoirs described it as 'the grit in the Whitehall oyster designed to produce a harvest of pearls'.[9] The CPRS was originally conceived more as a policy unit that would operate out of Number 10, but Heath's preference was that it should report to the Cabinet as a whole. It was led by Victor Rothschild, a former top biologist, MI5 agent, Chairman of the Agricultural Research Council and finally Vice-Director of scientific research at Shell, who was known for his left-leaning views. Much of the success of the 'Think-Tank', as Heath preferred to call it, is credited to the inspired appointment of Rothschild. The CPRS team was made up of high-flying civil servants seconded from departments and highly intelligent outsiders hand-picked from universities and the world of business. The unit had an average age of 35 and included William Waldegrave at the young age of 25 who would later go on to serve in Heath's private office and then go into Parliament. Heath regarded the think-tank as *one of the best innovations of my years at No. 10.*[10]

Not everyone was a fan of the think-tank, however. Burke Trend, the Cabinet Secretary, was particularly concerned that he would be left unable to influence the thinking of the unit, and Heath recounts one occasion on which Trend brought the first report of the CPRS to him having rewritten it. Heath requested the original report and proceeded to circulate that instead finding it *infinitely more effective*. This did not prevent the CPRS from fulfilling its role, however, and Rothschild set about writing provocative memos and forward-thinking reports. One innovation which must have seemed very modern to the grey politicians sitting round the Cabinet table was the use of oral presentations accompanied by visual aids and illustrative graphs. Here perhaps was the birth of the management consultant style we see so much of in government presentations today. Presentations to the Cabinet were meant to take place every six months, though in fact the CPRS only made it three times. Douglas Hurd described them as 'extraordinary occasions' where members of Rothschild's team 'rubbed Ministers' noses in the future'.[11]

Whether the CPRS contributed significantly to the government's direction, however, has been questioned. In particular, blame has been laid at its door for being the organisation responsible for leading Heath away from its election-winning strategy and into the U-turns which characterised the final years of government. It is true that the CPRS was highly supportive of statutory price setting which Heath eventually adopted despite outright opposition previously, but it is unlikely however that even if the CPRS had advised against such a course of action, Heath would have been able to withstand the pressure he was facing from within his party and the press. The CPRS became more involved with economic policy as the government progressed. In particular it put forward principles for discerning what constituted a 'lame duck' industry and argued that the government should make more efforts to let nationalised industries run themselves. The one inquiry which probably cemented its reputation for divining the future was into energy policy in 1973. Rothschild conjured up a scenario which predicted that the price of oil would rise from $1.90 a barrel to as much as $9 by 1985. Ministers may have been unbelievers at the time, but when the oil crisis struck just a short time later they were bowled over by the prescience of the report's findings even though it was 12 years out.

At the time when the CPRS might have been able to come into its own, however, it was sidelined because of a row between Rothschild and Heath. In the autumn of 1973 Rothschild made a doom-laden speech about the state of the economy on the same day that Heath made a speech saying the exact opposite. The headlines the next day carried Rothschild's message plunging the Prime Minister into embarrassment. Heath plays down the incident in his autobiography saying that after a strong rebuke any difficulty was all over in a few days, but a seminar planned by the CPRS was subsequently cancelled and Rothschild was no longer consulted. From then on, despite existing for another nine years, the think-tank lost its lustre and was finally abolished by Margaret Thatcher whose Policy Unit in 10 Downing Street was packed with people placed there to reinforce her thinking, not challenge it. Hurd lamented its passing, wondering whether it might have prevented the 'dangerous erosion of responsible cabinet government' had it survived.[12]

A reincarnation of the CPRS could be said to exist today in the Prime Minister's Strategy Unit which was set up in 2002 to develop policy to address long-term and cross-cutting issues. Full of secondees from McKinsey and other think-tanks as well as high-flying fast-track civil servants, the Strategy Unit may be its modern-day equivalent. Uncomfortable as it may be for both, there is a sense that Tony Blair is the prime minister Ted Heath would have liked to have been – a moderniser, pro-European, keen to shake-up Whitehall complacencies, a constitutional and welfare reformer, and a bridge between different communities, economically, socially and ethnically. Blair had combined Gladstone's interventionism and fiscal detail with Disraeli's sense of possibility and ear for change in the social composition and cultural priorities of the country. The group Ted Heath helped found first met before he was born, but Tony Blair is the first One Nation prime minister Britain has had.

Chapter 10: Mrs T Arrives

Andrew Roth, the formidable American-born parliamentary writer, concluded his compact but well-researched book, *Heath and the Heathmen*, which came out in 1972, at a time when Heath appeared to be getting over early troubles and hitting his stride with the prediction that 'Heath was sure he would have the last laugh at the end of the decade beginning in January 1973, during which he would help put Britain at the head of a West European super-power able to stare down either the Americans *or* the Russians.'[1]

Roth's view of the potential longevity of Heath and Heathism is a useful corrective to the later school of history, written often through eyes smitten by Thatcherism, that the Heath years were doomed to failure and were just a ghastly prelude to the arrival of a radiant, revolutionary leader. Heath was blown off course by a succession of events in 1973 over which he had no control like the Yom Kippur War, the massive rise in oil prices, the continuing instability in international politics and economics, and the failure of Europe to provide the stimulus to growth and modernisation that UK entry in January 1973 was meant to benefit from. He also made his own mistakes, not least misjudging the need for a general election in February 1974. 'With a little more patience,' wrote Jack Jones in 1986, 'he might still be leader of the Tory Party today ... Those of us who had got to know him well felt keen disappointment when he lost the leadership of his party ... Over the years he revealed a human face of Toryism, at least to union leaders who met him frequently. It is doubtful whether the public gained that view of him, partly because, as he himself admitted at one of the Downing Street meetings, he was a bad communicator. Amazingly, he gained more personal respect from union leaders than they seemed to have for Harold Wilson or even Jim Callaghan.'[2]

In 1974, I campaigned with great enthusiasm for a Labour victory in those bitterly cold February days. There was a grim slogging enthusiasm to get rid of Heath – the author of all national woes, so it seemed to young Labour activists. But the election was not fought on left-right lines. As Ben Pimlott accurately observed 'The Left had wanted a new socialist crusade. Instead, Wilson presented himself as a Labour Baldwin whom the voters could trust not to get into a flap.'[3] Arthur Scargill, Jack Jones, Hugh Scanlon and other aggressive trade union leaders went into purdah. They would keep their venom and vigour to destroy the next government – their own. The TUC kept saying the election was unnecessary and if only the Prime Minister were a bit more reasonable, a little less continental in wanting clear rational solutions to messy complex problems then Heath could get the miners back to work, the three-day week called off, electricity flowing and peace restored in workplaces. Heath found the enemy he wanted voters to vanquish had either walked off the battlefield or was successfully portraying itself as a group of reasonable men and women on poor salaries who just wanted to live in a fairer Britain. Instead of Heath-bashing Wilson talked emolliently about a social contract with the TUC which reasonable men and women could hardly object to.

For a whole weekend, Wilson stopped campaigning to

allow Enoch Powell to plunge his dagger into a Conservative prime minister's chest. The *Daily Mirror* published a centre-page consisting entirely of tiny crosses – each representing a miner who had been killed at work. Unfair but brutally effective propaganda. The *Daily Mail* by contrast splashed its front page on election day with the headline, 'A Handsome Win for Heath'. I walked the streets of Birmingham holding the paper up to see it greeted with catcalls and abuse as Lord Rothermere's boosterism for Heath proved counter-productive and, in the event, untrue. Prime Ministers who call elections when daylight is in short supply deserve the result they get. Heath's appeal for voters to make clear their views was left unanswered.

The Conservatives won 230,000 more votes than Labour which enjoyed its lowest share of the national vote since 1931, but Labour had 301 seats compared to 297 for the Conservatives. The surprise winners in vote terms were the Liberals who won an extra 4.5 million votes. With 19 per cent of the votes, compared to 37.9 per cent for Heath and 37.1 per cent for Wilson, Britain's first-past-the-post election system meant winners in terms of votes became losers as the Liberals only had 14 seats. The Ulster Unionists had 11 seats but the new leaders were William Craig and Ian Paisley who hated Heath. His handling of Northern Ireland had in effect dissolved the link between Conservatives on the mainland and Unionists in Ireland. Britain was moving into uncharted territory of the end of two-party politics. Heath spoke to Jeremy Thorpe, the Liberal leader, and offered him a post in the Cabinet plus a Speaker's conference on electoral reform, but even with the Liberal votes Heath would not have a clear Commons majority. Thorpe told Heath that he had clearly been rejected by voters. The statesmanlike option would have been to resign at once and allow another Conservative, unencumbered by all the dislikes Heath had engendered, to see if a majority could be formed.

Instead Britain was treated to the pathetic sight of its Prime Minister camping in Downing Street and waiting to see if the Liberals would give him a life-line. They would not and Wilson kissed hands for the third time on the Monday after the election. The defeat was a shock for Heath. He had no home and had to camp in a small flat south of the Thames. Instead of working out what was needed to re-invent the Conservative Party he continued on a business as usual basis. Around him top and junior Conservatives were unleashing an intellectual renewal of the party and turning it away from the post-war welfare state, mixed economy consensus. Keith Joseph launched the Centre for Policy Studies with the central European *émigré*, Alfred Sherman, as its director. Sherman had trained as a Marxist and spent time in Marxist politics. The United States is full of former communists, Trotskyists, and other Marxist intellectuals who switch to right-wing politics, because ultimately staying a Marxist in a democracy is to deny any chance of exercising power or, at least, influence over those who will win office. However, the kind of intense analytical ideological thinking and pleasure in seeking radical solutions to any economic and social problem which is the hallmark of Marxists means that when they transfer allegiance to the right, they cut through the mushy, middle-way compromise solutions that the Macmillan-Heath post-war Tories had stood for. William Waldegrave, the young All Souls intellectual, and like Heath, a former President of the Oxford Union, published a short book, *'Taming the Leviathian*, in this period and its title, with the implication that the task of modern Toryism was to reduce the role of the state in every sphere of British life, summed up the new mood.

Heath did not really sense these tectonic shifts in ideological thinking. His most obvious challenger with the ideological and political authority, and ministerial experience to be an alternative leader, Enoch Powell, had ruled himself out of mainstream politics by his decision not to fight the election and to urge a Labour vote. It is ideas that change first before new men or women emerge to articulate these ideas. In 1974, Heath was living on borrowed time. He had the model of Harold Wilson who was badly defeated in 1970 but stayed on as party leader and eventually returned to Downing Street. But was Wilson an example Heath wanted to imitate? Heath was struck by personal tragedy in September 1974 when his boat, *Morning Cloud*, was sunk and his godson was one of two crewmembers who were drowned. 1974 was an *annus horriblis* for Heath. Labour poured oil on the troubled waters of industrial relations and the country breathed with relief that the bruising confrontations of the Heath era appeared to be over.

An era which began with the Conservatives after 1945 accepting the new contours of a Whitehall-directed Britain was coming to an end. But politicians are often the last to know what is going on. Heath decided to go on. He fought the October 1974 election with little to offer voters. He rejected the call of proportional representation which if introduced in Britain on a purely proportional basis of seats allocated on the basis of national share of votes would result in the fissure of both the Conservative and Labour Parties into rival groups and open the way to the entry of fascist, racist and other populist or ethnic-based parties into the Commons. Instead he called for a 'National coalition government' to bring together all parties. This appeal to the spirit of 1931 found little echo. I was Labour candidate in the safe Conservative seat of Solihull in October 1974 and there was a joyous sense of finally getting rid of Heath once and for all. It did not really happen. Wilson was given a tiny majority of three. The two elections of 1974 settled nothing and the country limped though the rest of the 1970s aware that change was needed and that neither of the men born in 1916, Harold Wilson or Ted Heath, let alone the older Jim Callaghan could deliver it.

Having lost three elections out of four, Heath could not reasonably have expected to lead the Conservatives in a fifth contest. Yet he refused to go. Conservative MPs from every corner of the party were meeting, some openly, some in cabals, but all were united in the need for a change. The obvious challenger from the right was Sir Keith Joseph, the elegant, tortured intellectual Leeds MP who had been making right-wing speeches since the summer. Joseph allowed his logic to go too far with a eugenicist call for lower-class women to stop having babies in order to improve the national stock. His main supporter and, by her own admission, 'informal campaign manager' had been Margaret Thatcher. 'I had no doubt that Ted now ought to go. He had lost three elections out of four. He himself could not change and he was too defensive of his own past record to see that a fundamental change of policies was needed.'[4]

With Keith Joseph out of the race, Margaret Thatcher decided to challenge Heath. Her supreme advantage was that she had no clear ideological profile. She had been an utterly competent minister, cleaving to Whitehall estab-

'I had no doubt that Ted now ought to go. He had lost three elections out of four. He himself could not change and he was too defensive of his own past record to see that a fundamental change of policies was needed.'

MARGARET THATCHER

lishment truisms and forcing more grammar schools to become comprehensive schools than any other Education

Secretary. She was a grammar-school Oxford graduate from a middling background and thus had some parallel to Heath. But Heath's world view had been formed by the failures of right-wing politics in the 1920s and 1930s, while hers was shaped by the problems a statist, welfarist, corporatist Britain confronted and was unable to solve after her entry into the Commons in 1959. Unlike Heath, who had never owned a house, she married a very wealthy businessman and had a country house in addition to a Chelsea home. Certainly there was a hint of the Right about her. She had removed free school milk in order to control her department's budget but with the affluence of Britain in the 1970s it was hard to justify maintaining the provision of tiny bottles of milk in playgrounds which dated back to wartime. However, this measure, which mixed anti-working class meanness with tough control of tax-payer's money, appealed to the angry middle class *Daily Mail* Tories who hated Wilson, felt let down by Heath, and had no obvious champion. 'There is a widespread feeling in the country that the Conservative Party had not defended [Conservative] ideas explicitly and toughly enough, so that Britain is set on a course towards inevitable socialist mediocrity. That course must not only be halted, it must be reversed,' she said as her campaign got under way.[5] It was not just an attack on Heath but on the core ideology of post-war Conservativism. It thrilled the Right who moved to back her massively. In her autobiography, Mrs Thatcher presents herself almost as an outsider who took on and defeated the entire Conservative establishment. This is nonsense. She won precisely because she was seen as a perfect establishment figure. She had been a loyal, competent, unflashy, minister under three Conservative Prime Ministers. She did not seek cheap media exposure. Her name was not mentioned as a plotter or player in internal Tory politics in the 1960s or in Heath's government. She was a safe, centrist pair of hands. She was pro-European. Why not give her a chance?

Heath's campaign was a shambles. At one dinner organised by his supporter Kenneth Baker, the new young MP Lynda Chalker was present. As a pro-EEC, liberally-inclined young woman she was a natural for One Nation Heath. As Baker sought to persuade his guests to back Heath there came a moment in the dinner when his wife announced that the ladies should now leave to let the men get on with serious politics. The barely disguised sexism in Heath's campaign against Thatcher was counter-productive. She was no supporter of women's issues, let alone influenced by the growing ideas and movements associated with feminism. But she was a woman, married, with children at school or college. Somehow a further period of having the confirmed bachelor Heath who was oblivious to the new society of post-1968 Britain would have left the Tories still further out-of-touch with a changing Britain. Mrs Thatcher at least had some links via her children, her role as mother and wife, to the new world the baby-boom generation was shaping. Heath could have broken with the Tory past by resigning after the election defeat in October 1974. Instead, the Tories broke with him by electing Margaret Thatcher four months later in place of Heath. It was a new beginning for the Conservatives and, in due course, for the country. It was the end of Ted Heath's life as front-bencher after a quarter of a century and party leader for nine years. *The Times* published a leader praising Heath. 'He has served his party and his country honourably and with great energy and determination. His work in Europe has been his greatest achievement ... He has many of the qualities of a great man and has deserved the gratitude of his country.'

Chapter 11: Ted's Nemesis

Politics is personality. If politics, power and government were the application of designed theory mixed with decisive administration resulting in solutions no-one would take any interest. But far more important than ideas is the human passion of politics. For MPs in the Commons tea-room, bars and dining rooms the discussion focuses far more on human ambitions and foibles than the contents of a white paper or the nostrums of Oxbridge political philosophers.

Heath's personality remains an enigma. The kissing never started for him. Priapic politicians abound. Sometimes like John Profumo, Cecil Parkinson, or more lately Ron Davies and Boris Johnson are caught and serious career damage is done. On the other hand, Lloyd George's goatish behaviour was no bar to high office. John Major's passionate affair with his fellow MP and junior minister, Edwina Currie, was kept secret until both had left Parliament. Many politicians however sublimate all their passions into politics, at best entering into a token marriage to have the correct profile as parent and head of household. In the case of Heath, he does not seem to have had any sexual relationship of any sort. Even when best man at the marriage of his brother John, he avoided kissing the bride. Reporters who tracked girl companions in the 1930 and 1940s reported only platonic relationships. Heath would holiday with other MP friends, motoring all over Europe, and refusing to share the driving as if having his hands on the wheel and pumping up and down on the clutch was a form of physical outlet. His passion pumped through his fingers into the organ and piano. 'Music remained his great relaxation,' wrote his biographer, John Campbell, 'a source of spiritual refreshment which engaged parts of his personality which the daily life of politics did not. Those who heard these soul-cleansing performances at the end of a hard day have testified they could never again imagine Heath to be a cold man lacking in deep feeling.'[1] Heath discovered sailing aged 50. Like other men who solve their mid-life crisis by doing something intensely physical, like running marathons or trekking in the Himalayas, Heath enjoyed almost a carnal thrill as he threw his boats about the waves.

To the public this intense man came over simply as the new form of management-by-objectives politician. But underneath lay the old demons of personal rivalry which in the case of Heath rose up to devour him. His nemesis was Enoch Powell. There was a superficial similarity between the two men. Both born to modest families. Both grammar school boys. Both Oxbridge scholars. Both speaking an English distinct from the BBC Oxford norms of their party. Both went from grammar school to Oxford (Heath) and Cambridge (Powell). Although the Brummie was the academic star, the east Kent student left university having gained the confidence that comes with being President of the Union. Both went into the Army and worked mainly as staff rather than fighting officers, though Heath saw action in northern Europe.

Both entered the Commons in the 1950s and came together to form the One Nation group of young reformers who understood the need for ideas and new thinking to recreate a Conservative Party fit to govern the modernising Britain of the 1950s. Both quickly arrived on the front bench and attracted good notices from the press and their parliamentary colleagues. The similarities, however, ended almost as soon as they began their respective parliamentary careers. Powell would not join Heath, Churchill, Macmillan and Eden in a vote to support the Schuman plan. Heath was pro-European whereas Powell, in his first conscious act as an MP, displayed not only indifference to the traditional Conservative virtues of obeying the whip but a rejection of the growing enthusiasm of the Churchill-Macmillan Tories for Europe.

Heath as a junior whip had to deal with Powell rebelling over Suez. In his fine biography of Enoch Powell, the historian and polemicist Simon Heffer declares that Powell always believed 'the principal aim of America's foreign policy in the 20th century had been solely to diminish the power of others, including her nominal allies, to establish herself as a leading world power'. Powell's hostility, bordering on contempt, for the United States was consistent.[2] So in 1956 Powell voted against the withdrawal of British troops from Egypt as the American President Eisenhower forced Eden to retreat from the Suez adventure.

Powell then resigned as a Treasury Minister in 1957 in protest with his two more senior colleagues at the public spending laxity of the new Prime Minister, Harold Macmillan. For Macmillan, and later for Heath, governments should spend money, even at the price of deficits and inflation, to keep at bay the evils of unemployment which converted Macmillan to Keynesian interventionism in the 1930s. For Powell, a proto-monetarist, this was heresy. No government should spend more than it received and governments should strictly control the supply of money to stop inflation taking off even if millions of families were reduced to poverty or dependence on social security. Powell, an economic neoliberal, remorseless in following his logic wherever it went, hostile to Europe, contemptuous of America, a romantic about the empire, indifferent to the clubbish Commons obedience to whips had become a very difficult political animal to Heath by the time of the two-year long Tory crisis of 1963–5 when the party went through three leaders, lost an election and began a lengthy identity crisis which it has yet to resolve.

Powell was at the epicentre of this crisis. Indeed, for many he <u>was</u> the crisis. Heath's failure to deal with Powellism contributed to his own failure a decade later. It was not just a growing clash of personalities. Powellism was an alternative radical challenging Toryism that contained important truths even if presented in a fashion which alienated many. Powell's endless protestations that he was neither racist nor isolationist nor indifferent to the side effects of monetarism rang hollow then and ring hollow now from a man of such intellect. Powell had been a member of the Cabinet which had supported Britain's entry into the European Economic Community which Heath sought to negotiate at the beginning of the 1960s. As Health Minister he also presided over a policy of massive recruitment of nurses, doctors and other NHS staff from the Indian subcontinent and Britain's former colonies in the Caribbean. Thus, when he later chose to make the question of immigrants and Europe the battering ram against Edward Heath's leadership of the Conservative Party it was difficult to avoid the accusations of insincerity.

Powell stood in the 1965 leadership contest and gathered a derisory 15 votes. Nonetheless, Heath offered him one of the Conservative Party's most prized shadow cabinet portfolios, that of being defence spokesman. Straight away Powell went on the offensive, calling for Britain to pull out of Asia and like de Gaulle was openly indifferent to the American efforts to shore up a non-communist government in South

Vietnam. American diplomats started to protest to Heath about Powell's anti-Americanism.

For Heath, Powell became even more of a nuisance as he ranged far and wide over economic and social policy. He attacked Labour's move to incomes policy and criticised the tentative efforts of the Wilson government to promote reform of industrial relations. Powell's solution was simple. If the economy was deprived of money to pay the inflationary wage demands of trade unions then these demands could not be met and there would be no inflation. It was wrong to blame trade unions for acting in their own natural interests when controlling money supply would achieve the object of bringing down inflation immediately. That side effect might be mass unemployment and poverty was not something of any interest to Powell but to other Conservatives, still sensitive to what they perceived to be the Disraeli tradition of accepting social responsibility, the price of fighting inflation with monetarism was one they baulked at paying. Powell also criticised Tory policy on pensions and Heath's guarded support for the Labour government's attempts to deal with the unilateral declaration of independence in Rhodesia. Powell attacked the Bank of England and Heath's mentor, Harold Macmillan, in a scathing review of the former Prime Minister's first volume of memoirs. In 1967 he called for an end to a fixed exchange rate to allow the pound to float.

Yet he still voted with Heath in the lobby to support Harold Wilson's bid to get Britain into the Common Market, which was again wrecked by de Gaulle's refusal to countenance Britain as a full European partner. For Heath, the new leader of the Conservative Party trying to weld his Shadow Cabinet team into an effective opposition, Powell's incessant forays into every other sphere of public government and opposition policy were intolerable. Powell told a journalist that he deliberately included 'at least one startling assertion in every speech in order to attract enough attention to give me a power base within the Conservative Party. Providing I keep this going, Ted Heath can never sack me from the shadow cabinet.'[3] Heath himself wrote of Powell: *My long-standing view was that he was incurably eccentric but I still hoped he would honour his promise to stay clear of controversy. My hopes were misplaced.*[4]

My long-standing view was that he [Powell] was incurably eccentric but I still hoped he would honour his promise to stay clear of controversy. My hopes were misplaced.

HEATH

Then on 20 April 1968 Powell detonated his own bomb which took him off the front bench forever and made him the alternative leader of the British Right to Ted Heath. In a speech in his native Birmingham he appealed to every racist instinct of his audience of Conservative activists. Powell confirmed their prejudices by telling them that Britain's white population 'found themselves made strangers in their own country. They found their wives unable to obtain hospital beds in childbirth, their children unable to obtain school places, their homes and neighbourhoods changed beyond recognition.' He then referred to a constituent. 'She is becoming afraid to go out. Windows are broken. She finds excreta pushed through her letterbox. When she goes to the shops she is followed by children, charming, wide-grinning piccaninnies. They cannot speak English, but one word they know. "Racialist," they chant.' Powell's language then rose to new heights of populist demagogy. The decision that allowed immigrants into Britain, which he had certainly not objected to when that policy was adopted in the 1950s and 1960s to meet the demand for cheap labour especially in Britain's public services, meant that Britain now 'must be mad, literally mad, to allow family reunions of British immigrants to take place.

It is like watching a nation busily engaged in heaping up its own funeral pyre … . as I look ahead I am filled with foreboding. Like the Roman, I seem to see 'the River Tiber foaming with much blood.'"[5]

This apocalyptic vision unleashed a wave of racial hatred never before seen in Britain. Powell protested until his dying day that he was no racist. But the language about "piccaninnies" and the fact that no journalist could ever find the woman in Wolverhampton through whose letterbox Powell said shit had been pushed as well as the images he created of rivers foaming with blood and burning pyres constituted a vindication and validation of every anti-black passion that was tucked away in the inner recesses of many British hearts and minds. Tony Benn noted that in the days after Powell's speech 'two hundred dockers came to the House of Commons and shouted obscene things at Labour MPs and called Ian Mikardo a "bloody Chinese Jew". He recognised some of the East End fascist leaders amongst these guys. The white trash have picked this speech up. It has suddenly liberated them and there are strikes all over the place in support of Enoch Powell. He has really opened Pandora's box.'[6] For members of the Shadow Cabinet it was too much. They phoned up Heath and insisted that Powell had to go. Heath issued a statement describing the speech as *racialist in tone and liable to exacerbate racial tensions*, and he was therefore dismissing Powell from the Shadow Cabinet.

For his remaining six years as a Conservative MP Powell showed Heath no mercy. Heath was willing to support reform of the House of Lords when this was proposed by the Labour government. Powell opposed this. He created along with Michael Foot, a fellow traditionalist about Parliament, a campaign of parliamentary opposition which stopped the efforts to reform the Lords dead in their tracks. Powell now openly supported the racialist government headed by Ian Smith in Rhodesia and said that Britain should recognise Rhodesia as an independent republic. When troubles broke out in Northern Ireland Powell insisted that border controls should be instituted so that Irish citizens, who had always been able to travel freely to Britain despite being citizens of a foreign country, should no longer be able do so.

In the 1970 election Powell said that Britain faced three great dangers. The first he defined as immigration, calling for a policy of voluntary repatriation. The second was any question of entering the Common Market and the third was the level of taxation and state ownership. These themes appealed to a large number of Conservative voters. But overall Powell produced a reaction amongst many British citizens who were not white. They instinctively moved their votes and political enthusiasm to any candidates who were not tainted by Powellism. But Powell by now seemed almost indifferent to the fate of the Conservative Party. His objective was to get Heath. One of the more popular creations of the Churchill era of Conservative politics had been the United Nations. Writing about its 25th anniversary Powell dismissed the UN as a 'superstition ... The United Nations is, always has been, and always will be, an absurdity and a monstrosity, which no lapse of time and no application of ingenuity or effort can remedy'.[7] Then when Heath appointed John Davis, who had been the Director General of the CBI as his Trade and Industry Secretary, Powell compared the appointment to Caligula making his horse a consul. He continued to criticise the United States and when asked about the Commonwealth said, 'there is no such thing'. He claimed in 1971 that without his interventions, 'Edward Heath would not be Prime Minister and there would still be a Socialist Government in office.'

Powell linked up with anti-European Labour MPs like Michael Foot, Peter Shore and Tony Benn to create a wave smashing against Heath's desire to see Britain join the European Community. He was the only Conservative MP to vote with Labour when a censure motion was moved in the Commons in a technical row over what amendments could be added to the bill. Powell as a superb parliamentarian enjoyed using every procedural wrangle to trip up his own Tory government. He continued to oppose Heath's policy on Ireland, voting against the decision to impose direct rule. Although the Left, which was gaining authority in trade unions through militant organisation and strike activity was now firmly anti-Powellite, the Wolverhampton MP continued to attack the efforts of the Heath government to reform industrial relations or create an incomes policy. Yet while Powell's postbag was far greater than any other politician at the time he was unable to change the thinking of the Heath government. His attacks on Heath became more bitter and personal. In 1972, he said Heath had 'taken leave of his senses'[8] over his decision to create a prices and incomes policy.

Powell began to hint that the Labour Party, whose position was still hostile to Britain's entry into Europe and which had announced a policy of holding a referendum on Common Market membership, might be preferable in office than Edward Heath who had sought to uphold parliamentary sovereignty by insisting that the Commons should take the decision to sign the intergovernmental treaty which meant Britain entered into its new relationship with other countries in Europe. For Powell the populist, parliamentary sovereignty could be thrown overboard if there was a chance of organising a plebiscite which would deliver the policy he wanted, which was to maintain Britain's isolation from Europe. At the Conservative Party conference in 1973 Anthony Barber, the Chancellor of the Exchequer and close friend of Heath, described Powell as a 'frustrated fanatic'. The tensions between the failing Heath government about to enter its final confrontation with the miners and the general election in February 1974 and Powell were boiling out into the open. Powell described Heath's criticism of the miners' strike as an 'outburst ... one cannot but entertain fears for the mental and emotional stability of a head of government to whom such language can appear rational'.[9] Powell was no friend of trade unions or working people but simply objected to any efforts to control wages and prices. Implying Heath was mentally unstable – in plain English that the Prime Minister was mad – said more about Powell's mental state as he continued to be obsessed with the Tory sitting in Downing Street.

As 1974 opened and the hints grew that Heath might call an election Powell declared 'it would be fraudulent – or worse – to fight an election on the cry of "who governs the country?"'[10] And then when Heath called the election Powell delivered the blow that certainly helped hand power to Labour. I was a BBC political reporter in the West Midlands in this election period. Powell was very popular with white voters in Birmingham, the Black Country and Wolverhampton. But he also provoked an equal and opposite reaction from young political activists, like myself, who turned in increasing numbers to trade union and Labour Party work to stop as we saw it the political validation of the racist Britain that Powell's policy, whether intended or not, would bring into being in our judgement. The fillip to the Labour cause by the announcement that Powell could not stand in election and his statement, 'I personally cannot ask electors to vote for policies which are directly opposite to those which we all stood for in 1970', was the death-knell for Heath's hopes of retaining power. As Powell's biographer Simon Heffer writes, 'it seemed to him a matter of national urgency that Heath was removed from office and replaced by someone who could reopen the question of British membership of the EEC; and he intended to do all he could to bring that about'.[11] He entered into a secret conspiracy with Harold Wilson so that the two men would time their speeches so that Heath would face a double broadside during the election. Wilson and other senior Labour leaders stayed silent when Powell made a weekend speech to 1,500 people in Birmingham making clear that the pledge of the Labour Party to offer a referendum on European Community membership overrode any question of party loyalty. Shortly afterwards the press were informed that Powell had already voted, by post, for the Labour Party. Later Powell would claim, with justice, that he had cost Heath the office of Prime Minister in 1974.

Never before in British political history had two prominent figures within the same party fallen out to such an extent that one was willing to use all his authority and hold over a group of voters to deny his own party the chance of staying in office. Divisions at the top of party politics are part of the fabric of Britain's party and parliamentary history. Tony Benn, whose friendship for Enoch Powell 'was as genuine and pleasant as it was possible to achieve in politics',[12] helped keep Labour in opposition over many years after 1979 with his relentless organised opposition to successive party leaders and their efforts to make Labour electable. But Benn never went as far as Powell in betraying his party and urging a vote for the opposition. A century before, Randolph Churchill broke with the Conservative Party of the 1880s on the question of Ulster and formed his own unionist grouping which helped bring the Liberals to power and make Liberalism the hegemonic force in British politics until in turn the Liberals broke apart after 1918.

But never before had one politician spent so much of his time and energy seeking to undermine in every possible way the authority, power and office of his own party leader and Prime Minister. Supporters of Enoch Powell liked to think that his policies were then put into effect by Margaret Thatcher. Yet she took Britain much more deeply into a union with other European countries when she took the Single European Act through the House of Commons. It involved a far greater transfer of power and sharing of sovereignty to the rest of the European Community than that which Heath achieved when he signed the Treaty of Rome in 1973 or any other changes in the intergovernmental treaties that bind European Union members together so far this century. It is true Mrs Thatcher allowed floating exchange rates and to a limited extent controlled money supply but she took no action to cut the share of state income the government takes and adopted none of Powell's policies to deal with immigration or the question of Ireland. Enoch Powell famously wrote that all political careers end in failure. He did all in his power to destroy Ted Heath's Conservative government and both men took the mutual enmity to the grave.

Part Three

THE LEGACY

Chapter 12: Final Years

After 1975, Heath spent a further 26 years in the Commons. More than half his time as an MP was spent after he lost office and then power as Conservative leader. Nearly a third of his autobiography is devoted to his life and views on politics after he lost power in 1974 and leadership of the Conservative Party the following year. Like Trollope he believed that 'to sit in the British Parliament should be the highest object of ambition of every educated Englishman.' He still sat on the front bench but just below the gangway only a metre or so from ministers as they came and went under Margaret Thatcher and John Major. When the Conservatives went into opposition in 1997 he heaved his by now considerable bulk across the floor to park himself in the same spot on the opposition benches. Liberal-Democratic leaders, Paddy Ashdown and Charlie Kennedy, sat down decorously beside Heath giving him space in the most prized seat in the Commons – the one Churchill had made his own – as if the former Tory leader represented a one-person opposition party himself.

In a sense he did. Although he went off to make money with some occult financial relationships with China, a country that Heath visited regularly, and which he never criticised despite egregious abuses of human rights at Tianamen Square, Heath remained above all a parliamentarian. In 1992, he became father of the House, an honorific title for the MP with the longest continuous years of service. Britain does not know what to do with ex-prime ministers and they rarely know what to do with themselves. Labour ones like Clement Attlee and Harold Wilson stayed on after their defeats in 1951 and 1970 and in Wilson's case returned to power. Conservative Prime Ministers have either disappeared into quiet retirement with their earldoms to write memoirs with an occasional foray back to make a big speech. Or in the case of Bonar Law, Balfour, Douglas-Home they returned as front-line Cabinet ministers, accepting that to ride on the roundabout of political fortune does not always guarantee riding forever on the biggest horse.

'He could not go down from being Prime Minister and serve under some other chief without acknowledging himself to have been unfit for the place he had filled.'

ANTHONY TROLLOPE, *THE PRIME MINISTER*

Heath did neither. Not yet 60 when Mrs Thatcher took over he became a born again back-bencher full of political energy to drive forward his version of One Nation Toryism. He gave Mrs Thatcher one conference – her first as leader in 1975 – free of a speech but thereafter he became the Conservative's Banquo turning up at conference after conference and making speech after speech attacking Thatcherism in barely disguised code. Mrs Thatcher never quite came to terms with Heath sitting balefully in the Commons.[1] Although after 1975 he wrote sturdy books on sailing and music and a put-downable autobiography, Heath never fully came to be at ease with English. In his autobiography he wrote of *the decimation of manufacturing industry, which lost over one-sixth of its capacity* without, it seems, realising a decimation is significantly less than a sixth. Peter Walker is praised for *sterling work in keeping* [Heathites] *on board*. Full employment is a *laudable objective*. The clichés roll out and on.

The Conservative Party likes its star politicians to write well. Disraeli and Churchill, were succeeded by *Spectator* editors like Ian Gilmour and Nigel Lawson or fine writers like Douglas Hurd and Chris Patten in Mrs Thatcher's government. This is actually a Continental tradition where good writing and essays into criticism, biography or history are seen as helpful to a political life. Labour briefly had proper writers like Roy Jenkins and Tony Crosland in high office but British politics has all but given up using language to convince. Heath wrote as he spoke in public, with a leaden pen to match a wooden tongue. As a result his critique of Thatcherism or Major's appeasement of anti-Europeans never resonated with a phrase or metaphor that commanded attention. The passion and scorn were there. Anyone who saw him in the House of Commons in his long, lonely years could almost feel the Vesuvian passions boiling below an impassive face. Occasionally he would rise and when interrupted by some whippersnapper of a Conservative MP willing to check him on matters European would turn with weary scorn to the Speaker's Chair to complain that *some people have no manners these days*.

The hates were there for all to see. At each party conference which he attended like a fusion between Banquo and the Ancient Mariner, he would offer a dinner to political editors. Once he was given a present as a thank-you by a woman journalist. He opened the box and found inside a chocolate face of Margaret Thatcher. In front of the journalists and the many other Conservative ministers dining at the restaurant he picked up his knife and smashed his female nemesis into smithereens. His friend Douglas Hurd wrote and warned him that his behaviour was doing Heath little good. 'I think you have quite enjoyed being a volcano on the edge of the plain, watching the tribesmen scurry about when you erupt but I wonder if that period shouldn't come to a close!'[2]

It never did. In 1979 Mrs Thatcher was a relative novice in foreign affairs. She had politely supported the 'Yes' campaign in the 1975 referendum on keeping Britain a member of the European Community but left the day-to-day campaigning to enthusiastic pro-Europeans like Heath, Roy Jenkins and Jo Grimond. Jimmy Carter was still president of the United States and European politics were dominated by Valery Giscard d'Estaing in France and Helmut Schmidt in Germany with Roy Jenkins promoting the role of European Commission president to the point where he was invited to the new G7 club as a world leader alongside the American president, and the heads of government from the big European states, Japan and Canada.

The new Prime Minister's turn to Euro-scepticism was a much later affair. In 1979, and in two subsequent elections, the Conservatives were the pro-EU party of British politics with Labour surrendering to the isolationist passions of Tony Benn, Peter Shore and Michael Foot. Jack Straw, a rising Labour MP, captured the anti-European mood of Labour when he accused Mrs Thatcher of 'hauling down the Union Jack and raising the white flag of surrender' when she reported to the Commons her agreement to an increase in the EU budget.

In 1979 there were no obvious reasons for Mrs Thatcher not to offer the post of Foreign Secretary to Heath. No other Conservative politician had the experience, the contacts, or authority to speak for Britain in Europe or around the world. Heath had worked with Willy Brandt on the North-South report though he found Brandt's enormous capacity for alcohol and indifference to orderly work hard to bear. The report's analysis and its acute linkage of poverty with environmental challenges and the turn to terrorism of the angry and excluded was ahead of its time. It added to Heath's portfolio of international awareness but its recommendations were not in sync with the new ideologies taking over in London and Washington.

Mrs Thatcher wrote a polite letter to Heath saying she would make Lord Carrington, a charming Old Etonian fox, her Foreign Secretary. His great achievement, helped by another Old Etonian smoothie, Christopher Soames, was to get the Rhodesian imbroglio out of British politics where it had exposed the weakness of successive British governments' inability to dismantle racist rule in the colony. It is hard to see Heath having the same ability to draw together into compromise the bitter enemies of Rhodesia, with as much hate and rivalry within the competing African political groupings as between the white and black leaders. As she gained in confidence, Mrs Thatcher, like most Prime Ministers, became her own Foreign Secretary. Even if Heath had taken the post it is hard to see him in harness with his nemesis. Instead she offered him the British Ambassadorship in Washington. This was where Churchill had dumped Lord Halifax after the then Foreign Secretary had lost out to Churchill to become Prime Minister in 1940. The title and the grand house cannot disguise the fact that being an ambassador in Washington was never again to be at the heart of major policy making. In a crisis, a good ambassador is a valuable asset to a Prime Minister. Top class diplomats build bridges that allow nations with competing interests to rub along together. Heath as a former Prime Minister would have been in a different class. He was hardly likely to have accepted the myriad of petty Whitehall controls and restrictions that are the bane of a modern ambassador's life. The offer of the ambassadorship was not so much a sop as an insult. It was Mrs Thatcher's way of effecting a rupture with her predecessor and left Heath the choice of submission or sulk. For the rest of his parliamentary life he chose the latter.

For Heath, the 1980s were *an aberration when a combination of economic and political circumstances, a divided centre-left, vast regional disparities in unemployment and changing working patterns seriously but temporarily unbalanced the political equation.*[3] He gave the Thatcher government little respite. In speech after speech in the Commons he criticised and complained. He did not seek to form a coherent anti-Thatcher group. Ian Gilmour recalls 'he always acted alone; he never caballed against her'. Gilmour contrasts Heath's behaviour to his successor's private and public attacks on her successor, John Major.[4] He made television programmes like some young left-winger to show up the folly of monetarism. Thatcher's Chancellor, Nigel Lawson, found himself challenged when Heath came up with an alternative budget in 1985. His critique of Thatcherism reads well. She created a desert in many regions of the country and called it peace. And yet, Heath, Macmillan and Wilson had all sought to govern Britain from the centre and apply the rationalities of Balliol PPE graduates to the stubborn resistance to modernisation, change and renewal that British capitalism, public services, education and institutions ranging from the professions to the unions and universities so obviously needed. Heath was unable to admit his own failure. The man who had a rigorous professional analysis for many problems was unable to analyse himself and invent a new Edward Heath for the 22 years he remained in the Commons after 1979. And Mrs Thatcher did what Heath did not – win three elections in a row.

Yet paradoxically a new Heath emerged. Ted became Sir Edward as he picked up the automatic Knighthood of the Garter that comes to retired prime ministers, but he waited until Mrs Thatcher left office to receive it in 1992. He became an Ambassador for communist China. In 1974, he gawped at the reception he received when thousands turned out to greet him when he first arrived in Beijing. Clearly he had no idea how easy it is to turn out tens of thousands in countries like China and India for the visit of even minor dignitaries. Mao Zedong and Zhou Enlai had him eating out of their hands with a little flattery and discussion of his political activity at Oxford. Occasionally newspapers would try to investigate how he managed to run a secretariat, fly with his own doctors on visits abroad, buy a large Queen Anne house in Salisbury and live in some style on his backbench MP's salary. Inquiries led to China but then hit an inscrutable wall.

The interventionist Conservative and staunch anti-Communist who accused Chamberlain of turning *all four cheeks* to European dictatorship quietly made his peace with tyranny, torture and intolerance. A visit to Iran convinced him that freedom of expression as practised by Salman Rushdie was going too far. Instead, the British novelist should apologise for the offence caused to Muslims. *We in the West must learn to be rather more cautious about judging the political arrangements in other parts of the world by our own subjective standards*, declared Heath. Such relativism and his support for the realist doctrine of non-intervention in the Balkans by John Major's government as Britain not only stood to one side but actively thwarted efforts by others to stop the Nazi-style mass murders of opponents by Slobodan Milosevic and Franjo Tudjman were a far cry from the Heath who stood in solidarity with the people of Spain and Germany against arbitrary arrests and death squads. Up to 1939, perhaps some 10,000 people had been killed by Nazi thugs in Germany. By 1995, the butchers of the Balkans had more blood on their hands. Despite this murderous assault on fellow Europeans Heath had nothing but scorn for those he dismissed as the *'something must be done'* brigade.[5]

To be fair, there is a legitimate argument for the realist

school of diplomacy. Its most supreme practitioner and best theoretician is Henry Kissinger. *The West as a whole, as well as his own country, owes an immense debt to him*, Heath argued though he was scornful of the German émigré Kissinger over what Heath considered to be his patronising handling of Europe. The far road Heath travelled from his interventionist 1930s to his realist 1990s was seen in his efforts to involve himself in the Iraq conflict after Saddam Hussein invaded Kuwait in 1990. Heath was invited by two of his protégés, Douglas Hurd and William Waldegrave, who were running the Foreign Office in the last months of the Thatcher government, to go to Baghdad and negotiate the release of dozens of British citizens who had been trapped in Iraq after the invasion and were seen as hostages. Mrs Thatcher vetoed the scheme when she heard about it. Heath ignored her opposition. He continued imperturbably with the help of the publicity-seeking Richard Branson who offered to fly out one of his planes to bring the trapped Britons home. The triple pleasure of high-profile international diplomacy, a genuine humanitarian objective, and the tweaking of the Thatcher tail made the initiative a perfect example of late Heathism in action. He took malicious pleasure in driving over from his Salisbury home to Bournemouth to call a press conference at the Conservative Party conference. As the Defence Secretary Tom King rose to speak in defence of the government's policy on Iraq, Heath was briefing the media in the gallery. The headlines the next day were again for Heath, not the government. Like his other nemesis, Enoch Powell, two decades previously, Heath now used the art of timing his press interventions to maximise embarrassment for his beleaguered party leader. He succeeded with his mercy mission, but Saddam in 1990 as in 2003 was happy to use western politicians who went out to Baghdad as messengers. Heath told him to withdraw from Kuwait but the visit by a former British Prime Minister to the tyrant caused great anger even among loyal Heath followers in the Conservative Party. Douglas Hurd and Michael Heseltine, two devoted Heathites on matters European, were bitter in their denunciations.

Heath's long period of internal exile never came to a happy political end. The Conservatives became more and more hostile to Europe. John Major's appeasement of what he called 'the bastards' – the hard core of Eurosceptic Cabinet ministers including John Redwood, Michael Howard and William Hague, helped lead the Conservatives to their worst-ever defeat. Heath's biography came out in 1998 and was a long litany of 'I told you so's' on Tory failures on Europe since he gave up the Leadership. Major's successors have been if anything more Eurosceptic to the point where the latest leader, David Cameron, wants to sever links with sister mainstream right-wing parties in European parliamentary politics and instead make alliances with the ultra-nationalistic, homophobic, and women-hating religious parties.

Again and again, Heath would rise in the Commons to speak on Europe and seek to make obvious points about the European Community and then Union. The Eurosceptic Conservative MP, Bernard Jenkin, son of Heath's cabinet member, Patrick Jenkin, says that Heath enjoyed the 1992 parliament enormously. 'Thatcher was gone. He had rows over Maastricht. He was the centre of attention again and he loved it.'[6] His arguments and facts on the EU were irrefutable (save to hardened anti-EU ideologues) his reasoning compelling, his stance within the main traditions of non-isolationist Toryism. But other than a dwindling band of men who still held on to One Nation Toryism no-one else listened. When Heath died in 2005 it was notable that Tony Blair paid a warmer tribute to Ted Heath than anyone from the Conservative front bench.

In 1999 Heath went to Aachen to watch Tony Blair being given the Charlemagne Prize for his services to Europe. Heath and one or two other elderly recipients of the annual award wore their Charlemagne prize medallions on their chests as the pro-European Blair received his reward, the orchestra played Beethoven's *Ode to Joy* and a German cardinal preached the virtues of European integration above the tomb where Charlemagne's remains lay. In 2003, when I was Europe Minister, I organised a lunch party in Heath's honour to commemorate Britain joining Europe. Past disciples like Douglas Hurd, Geoffrey Howe and Michael Heseltine came and gathered around him. He spoke seated down, without notes and still recalling the walk in the Elysée Garden – *without officials* – when he cut the deal with President Pompidou and took the decision which eluded his predecessors and made life awkward for his successors.

Tony Blair paid a generous tribute by video link. He had been at Oxford when Heath took Britain into Europe. Blair's first ever vote was in the referendum in 1975 when he voted Yes to Europe. Blair after 1997 was popular and well-received in Europe. His Cabinet had squeezed public Euroscepticism out of its DNA. Yet Britain after 1997 still found itself unable to take a decisive step towards Europe by signalling a willingness in principle to join the Euro, or to support other measures of greater integration. Blair's announcement that Britain would hold a referendum on the proposed European constitutional treaty made it all but impossible for France not to do the same. The decision was made for purely tactical reasons. Labour candidates faced a united clamour for a referendum from Conservatives, Liberal-Democrats, UKIP, the BNP and the nationalist parties. Difficult local, European and parliamentary elections beckoned. The Foreign Secretary, Jack Straw, an acute and seasoned election campaigner, was supported by all but one of his ministerial team in urging a referendum and thus killed the populist campaign of the media, the Lib-Dems and other parties for a plebiscite on Europe. Like Harold Wilson giving in to Tony Benn's campaigning for a referendum in the 1970s, Blair was unable to resist the same appeal two decades later. France had to follow suit and the constitutional treaty was doomed. The French and the Dutch voted down the constitutional treaty shortly after Blair was returned to power with a reduced majority and a cabinet that was losing all enthusiasm for Europe. Heath died shortly afterwards, having been the only prime minister who had been willing not just to say nice words about Europe but actually advance to a real risk-taking decision involving leadership based on principle and belief.

The flamboyant right-wing Tory Alan Clark wrote of the early 1970s, 'During this period it can be asserted without fear of contradiction that the administration (though not the party) finally abandoned any claim to call itself Conservative.'[7] The experienced Tory MP and former minister, Ian Gilmour, disagreed. 'To attack Ted Heath for not having behaved like Margaret Thatcher is little more sensible than to say that the First World War could have been won more cheaply by using the methods of the second.'[8] Heath vs Thatcher is an argument that will never be settled as long as the Conservative Party exists. Yet, until the 21st century Tories do decide whether their future depends on a return to pure Thatcherism or a reworking of One Nation Toryism, they will remain a split, even schizophrenic political force.

The long period of Heath the backbench former Prime Minister was dominated by a return to almost boyish enthusiasm for the Commons. He was there for every Prime Minister's question time, key statements and debate. He sat impassively. As years went by his body got rounder, his ankles swelling in the comfortable shoes he wore. In the evening if a vote commanded his presence, he would wear a white tuxedo so that at every gathering he stood out from the crowd. He spoke well, usually without notes. At dinners in his honour on the embassy round he would get up and sparkle with wit, a sense of history, some venom and simple reaffirmation of his European creed. He opened exhibitions and launched musical events. His more formal speeches were delivered in a heavy speaking style. Prepared carefully, they had the hallmark of earnestness and homework but there is no memorable phrase to enter the lexicon of political quotations from Heath. It was part of a deliberate style to be seen as a heavyweight and keep in a very small-town English way all passion firmly under wraps. Yet as Thatcher and Major faded from view, with Wilson dead, and Callaghan now very old, Heath was still to be found up to his retirement from the Commons in 2001 as a serious major politician with the magic initials 'MP' after his name. He had made and lived more history than any other British politician in active service. Until the last he was very much part of Britain's political *actualité*.

Picture Sources

Page vi
Edward Heath photographed when he first entered the Cabinet in 1959. (Topham Picturepoint)

Pages 66–7
Upon his arrival at the Elysée Palace in Paris, Edward Heath is splattered with ink by Miss Karen Cooper in protest to his signing Britain into the Common Market, 24 January 1972. (Topham Picturepoint)

Notes

Chapter 1: Early Years

1. Ben Pimlott, *Harold Wilson* (Harper Collins, London: 1992) p 8.
2. John Campbell, *Edward Heath* (Jonathan Cape, London: 1993) p 3.
3. Edward Heath, *The Course of My Life* (Hodder and Stoughton, London: 1998) p 17, hereafter Heath, *Course*.
4. Heath, *Course*, p 24.
5. Quoted in Alan Clark, *The Tories* (Weidenfeld and Nicholson, London: 1998) p 309.
6. Interview with Lord Walker.
7. Private talk with Lord Patten.
8. Heath, *Course*, p 736.

Chapter 2: War and Into Parliament

1. Dermot Englefield, *Facts about the British Prime Ministers* (Mansell, London: 1995) p 329.
2. Andrew Roth, *Heath and the Heathmen* (Routledge, London: 1972) p 45.
3. Heath, *Course*, p 102.
4. See Edmund Dell, *The Schuman Plan and the British Abdication of Leadership in Europe* (Oxford University Press, Oxford: 1995).
5. Heath, *Course*, p 111.
6. Heath, *Course*, p 126.

Chapter 3: Rising Front-Bencher

1. Janet Morgan (ed), *The Backbench Diaries of Richard Crossman* (Hamilton and Cape, London: 1981) p 30.
2. Roth, *Heath and the Heathmen*, p 76 and Campbell, Edward Heath, p 80.
3. John Barnes and Richard Cockett, 'The Making of Party Policy', in Anthony Seldon and Stuart Bell (ed), *The Conservative Century. The Conservative Party since 1900* (Oxford University Press, Oxford: 1994) p 370.
4. Heath, *Course*, p 153.
5. John Major, *Autobiography* (HarperCollins, London: 1999) p 78.
6. Heath, *Course*, p 150.
7. Englefeld et al op cit, p 329.
8. Heath, *Course*, p 155.
9. Heath, *Course*, p 103.
10. Private information from the late Steve Walker, history teacher of genius at St Benedict's School, Ealing in the 1950s and 1960s and a friend of Reginald Maudling at Merton College, Oxford before the war.

11. Quoted in Campbell, *Edward Heath*, p 101.

12. Campbell, *Edward Heath*, p 106.

Chapter 4: Into Cabinet

1. See Alan Bullock, *Ernest Bevin: Foreign Secretary* (Heinemann, London: 1983) for a full discussion, and for details of the intra union and party struggle for ideological supremacy in post 1945 Britain see Denis MacShane, *International Labour and the Origins of the Cold War* (Oxford University Press, Oxford: 1992) pp 144–86.

2. Gallup poll quoted in Andrew Taylor, 'The Party and the Trade Unions' in Seldon and Ball (eds), *The Conservative Century*, p 518.

3. Andrew Taylor, 'The Party and the Trade Unions' in Seldon and Ball (eds), *Conservative Century*, p 517

4. Heath, *Course*, p 194.

5. Heath, *Course*, p 194.

Chapter 5: Into Europe and Party Leadership

1. John W Young, *Britain and European Unity, 1945–1992* (Macmillan, London: 1993) p 16.

2. Heath, *Course*, p 145.

3. Quoted in Heath, *Course*, p 147.

4. Heath, *Course*, p 145.

5. Young, *Britain and European Unity*, p 72.

6. Heath, *Course*, p 210.

7. Roth, *Heath and the Heathmen*, p 145.

8. Heath, *Course*, p 220.

9. Greg Rosen, *Old Labour to New* (Politicos, London: 2005) p 240.

10. Rosen, *Old Labour to New*, p 243.

11. Heath, *Course*, pp 226–7.

12. Young, *Britain and European Unity*, pp 79–80.

13. Roth, *Heath and the Heathmen*, p 166.

14. Campbell, *Edward Heath*, p 128.

15. Alain Peyrefitte, *C'était de Gaulle* (Paris Fayard, Paris: 1994) pp 154–63.

16. Peyrefitte, *C'était de Gaulle*, p 299.

17. Peyrefitte, *C'était de Gaulle*, p 348.

18. Heath, *Course*, p 235.

Chapter 6: Taking on Wilson

1. Anthony Sampson, *Anatomy of Britain Today* (Hodder & Stoughton, London: 1965) p 77.

2. Quoted in Campbell, *Edward Heath*, p 206.

3. Tony Benn, *Diaries 1963–1967* (Hutchinson, London: 1987) pp 345–6.

4. Quoted in Englefeld et al, op cit, p 329.

5. Robert Taylor in Ben Pimlott and Chris Cook (eds), *Trade Unions in British Politics: the first 250 years* (Longman, London: 1991) p 185.

6. Quoted in Campbell, *Edward Heath*, p 228.

7. Roth, *Heath and the Heathmen*, p 203.

8. Roth, *Heath and the Heathmen*, p 203.

9. Harold Wilson, *The Labour Government 1964–1970* (Weidenfeld and Nicholson, London: 1971) p 432.

10. David Butler papers, Nuffield College, Oxford, hereafter Butler Papers. I am grateful to Professor Butler for sight of his contemporaneous notes of interviews with Heath and other politicians of the period covered in this book.

11. Interview with Lord Walker.

12. Campbell, *Edward Heath*, p 265.

13. Butler Papers.

14. Butler Papers.

Chapter 7: Downing Street Years

1. Englefeld, op cit, p 129.

2. George Hutchinson, *Edward Heath, A Personal and Political Biography* (Longman's, London: 1970) p 152.

3. Butler papers.

4. David Marquand, *The Unprincipled Society* (Cape/Fontana, London: 1988) p 52.

5. Margaret Thatcher, *The Path to Power* (HarperCollins, London: 1995) p 207.

6. Henry Kissinger, *Years of Upheaval* (Weidenfeld and Nicholson, London: 1982) p 140.

7. Heath, *Course*, p 488.

8. Heath, *Course*, p 488.

9. Sir Christopher Soames to Sir Denis Greenhill (Permanent Under Secretary, Foreign and Commonwealth Office) 21 April 1971. Key documents obtained under the Freedom of Information Act are to be found on the website of the Margaret Thatcher Foundation.

10. See Edmund Dell, *The Schuman Plan and the British Abdication of Leadership in Europe* (Clarendon Press, Oxford: 1995) pp 190–214.

11. Quoted in Ben Pimlott, *Harold Wilson* (HarperCollins, London: 1992) p 590.

12. Jean-Marcel Jeanneney, 'Trois raisons contre l'adhésion de la Grande-Bretagne à la C.E.E.', *Le Monde*, 5 May 1971.

13. Secret Record of a Conversation between the Prime Minister and the President of the French Republic in the Elysée Palace, Paris, at 10.00 A.M. on Thursday 20 May 1971, hereafter Secret Record. Margaret Thatcher Foundation. It is deeply to be regretted that in preparing papers for release under the 30-year rule this important document was not put in the Public Record Office. Had I been Minister at the time I would have authorised its publication.

14. Heath, *Course*, p 488.
15. Secret Record.
16. See John Palmer, *Europe without America? The Crisis in Atlantic Relations* (Oxford University Press, Oxford: 1987) pp 142–3.
17. Heath, *Course*, p 372.
18. Quoted in Rosen, *Old Labour to New*, p 296.
19. Rosen, *Old Labour to New*, pp 300–1.
20. John W Young, *Britain and European Unity, 1945–1992* (Macmillan, London: 1993) p 117.
21. Campbell, *Edward Heath*, p 363.

Chapter 8: Industrial Relations and the Economy, 1970–4

1. Heath, *Course*, p 327.
2. Campbell, *Edward Heath*, p 308.
3. Richard Sennett, *The Culture of the New Capitalism* (Yale University Press, Yale: 2006) p 176.
4. Sennett, *The Culture of the New Capitalism*, p 177.
5. Jack Jones, *Union Man* (Collins, London: 1986) p 215.
6. Robert Taylor, 'The Trade Union "problem" in the age of Consensus 1960–1979', in Pimlott and Cook (eds), *Trade Unions in British Politics*, p 175.
7. Andrew Taylor, 'The Party and the Trade Union', in Seldon and Bell (eds), *Conservative Century*, p 522
8. Tony Benn, *Office Without Power, Diaries 1968–1972* (Hutchinson, London: 1988) p 392.
9. Quoted in Dennis Kavangh, *Thatcherism and British Politics. The End of Consensus?* (Oxford University Press, Oxford: 1987) p 72–3.
10. Jones, *Union Man*, p 257.
11. Taylor, 'The Party and the Trade Union', in Seldon and Bell (eds), *The Conservative Century*, p 526
12. Marquand, *The Unprincipled Society*, p 163.
13. Marquand, *The Unprincipled Society*, p 163.

Chapter 9: Ulster and Reform of Government

1. Campbell, *Edward Heath*, p 423.
2. Roth, Heath and the Heathmen, pp 233, 234.
3. Heath, *Course*, p 421.
4. PRO MoD file DEFE 24/714 'Northern Ireland: Operation Motorman'.
5. Heath, *Course*, p 438.
6. Campbell, *Edward Heath*, p 311.
7. Campbell, *Edward Heath*, p 314.
8. Heath, *Course*, p 315.
9. Douglas Hurd, *Memoirs* (Little, Brown, London: 2003) p 206.

10. Heath, *Course*, p 316.
11. Heath, *Course*, p 316.
12. Douglas Hurd, *An End to Promises* (Collins, London: 1979) p 39.

Chapter 10: Mrs T Arrives

1. Roth, *Heath and the Heathmen*, p 234.
2. Jones, *Union Man*, pp 261–2.
3. Pimlott, *Harold Wilson*, p 610.
4. Thatcher, *The Path to Power*, p 261.
5. Thatcher, *The Path to Power*, p 275.

Chapter 11: Ted's Nemesis

1. Campbell, *Edward Heath*, p 249.
2. Simon Heffer, *Like the Roman. The Life of Enoch Powell* (Weidenfeld and Nicholson, London: 1998). Readers are directed to the excellent index of Heffer's book which has dozens of references to Powell's anti-americanism.
3. Roth, *Heath and the Heathmen*, p 204.
4. Roth, *Heath and the Heathmen*, p 290.
5. Heffer, *Like the Roman*, pp 449–55.
6. Benn, *Diaries 1968–1972*, p 6.
7. Heffer, *Like the Roman*, p 571.
8. Heffer, *Like the Roman*, p 654.
9. Heffer, *Like the Roman*, p 683.
10. Heffer, *Like the Roman*, p 693.
11. Heffer, *Like the Roman*, p 701.
12. Heffer, *Like the Roman*, p 952.

Chapter 12: Final Years

1. Tony Benn, *Conflicts of Interest, Diaries 1977–1980* (Hutchinson, London: 1990) p 182.
2. Heath, *Course*, p 552.
3. Heath, *Course*, p 583.
4. Ian Gilmour, *The Conservatives* (Fourth Estate, London: 1997) p 358.
5. Gilmour, *The Conservatives*, p 627.
6. Conversation with Bernard Jenkin MP.
7. Alan Clark, *The Tories* (Weidenfeld and Nicholson, London: 1998) p 309.
8. Gilmour, *The Conservatives*, p 291.

Year	Premiership
1970	19 June: Edward Heath becomes Prime Minister, aged 53. National dock strike. BP discovers oil in the North Sea. Equal Pay Act
1971	May: Heath meets French President to negotiate EEC entry Northern Ireland death toll reaches 173. August: Internment begins in Northern Ireland. October: Heath wins Commons vote on EEC entry Industrial Relations Act. Decimal currency introduced.
1972	January: National coal strike. Number of unemployed exceeds 1 million. 'Bloody Sunday in Northern Ireland': Britain assumes direct rule. Entry to EEC Nationwide dock strike in Britain. Housing Finance Act Local Government Act.
1973	Disorder in Northern Ireland following detention of first Protestant terror suspects. Pay rises limited to £1 per week plus 4 per cent and later to 7 per cent or £2.25. Energy crisis prompts state of emergency. NUM rejects government pay deal.
1974	January: Direct rule of NI ends. Miners' strike begins. Three-day week introduced and state of emergency declared. 4 March: Heath leaves office after three years and 259 days.

History	Culture
US ground troops withdraw from Cambodia.	Richard Bach, *Jonathan Livingston Seagull*.
PLO hijack four aircraft.	The Beatles split up.
	Jimi Hendrix dies.
	Films: *Kes. Love Story. Ryan's Daughter*.
Idi Amin seizes power in Uganda.	Shostakovich, *Symphony No. 15*.
USA ends trade embargo with China.	Godspell, *Jesus Christ Superstar*.
Indo-Pakistan war: East Pakistan becomes Bangladesh.	Films. *A Clockwork Orange. Death in Venice. Sunday, Bloody Sunday*.
	TV: *The Two Ronnies. Upstairs Downstairs*.
Nixon is first US president to visit USSR.	Jacobs/Casey, *Grease*.
Watergate scandal begins.	Roxy Music, *Roxy Music*.
Arab terrorists murder 11 Israeli Olympic athletes in Munich.	Frederick Forsyth, *The Day of the Jackal*.
Nixon wins US presidential election.	V S Naipaul, *In a Free State*.
	Films: *Deliverance. The Godfather. Cabaret*.
	TV: *Emmerdale Farm. Mastermind*.
Watergate trial begins.	Mike Oldfield, *Tubular Bells*.
Vietnam cease-fire agreement signed in Paris..	Richard Adams, *Watership Down*.
Last US troops leave Vietnam..	Graham Greene, *The Honorary Consul*.
General Pinochet seizes power in Chile;	Peter Schaffer, *Equus*.
Yom Kippur War.	Films: *The Exorcist*.
	TV: *The Ascent of Man. The World at War. Last of the Summer Wine*.
Swedish monarchy is stripped of all its remaining powers.	John Le Carré, *Tinker, Tailor, Soldier, Spy*.
	Jeffrey Archer, *Not a Penny More, Not a Penny Less*.
	Abba, *Waterloo*, wins Eurovision Song Contest.
	Films: *Murder on the Orient Express*.
	TV: *The Naked Civil Servant*.

Further Reading

The succinct, easy-to-read, but objective, analytical and penetrating narrative of British politics in the period covered in this book has yet to be written. There are many fine biographies and less fine autobiographies. Heath kept all his papers but never kept a diary. His autobiography, *The Course of My Life* (Hodder and Stoughton, London: 1998) is the prime source. It is unusual in that unlike many politician's autobiographies it was written more than two decades after he left office and the party leadership. Although he settles plenty of scores in it, there is no reason to question its honesty and accuracy. John Campbell has written an authoritative biography, *Edward Heath* (Jonathan Cape, London: 1993), which is unlikely to be surpassed in narrative or good judgement. Andrew Roth, *Heath and the Heathmen* (Routledge, London: 1972), which is based on Roth's exhaustive and cross-referenced news-cuttings system. All three books have been used in preparing this short biography.

Douglas Hurd was close to Heath as an aide in the 1960s and up to 1974 and went on to a distinguished political career himself. His autobiography (*Memoirs* (Little, Brown, London: 2003)) catches the mood of the Heath years well.

The various diaries of contemporary politicians like Tony Benn or Richard Crossman tell us how Heath was seen at the time. To get a feel of the Tory Party in power in the era before Heath became leader, novels by Maurice Edelman are a good guide just as the deference to the consensual centrism of Whitehall which Heath admired can be found in the novels of C P Snow.

Simon Heffer's magnificent biography of Enoch Powell (*Like the Roman. The Life of Enoch Powell* (Weidenfeld and Nicholson, London: 1998) takes us into the heart of Toryism 1945–75, a different, more passionate, ideological, raw Toryism that co-existed alongside Heath's world but was not of it. Leaving personalities to one side, *The Conservative Century. The Conservative Party Since 1900* (Oxford University Press, Oxford: 1994), edited by Anthony Seldon and Stuart Ball, is a treasure trove for understanding how the Conservative Party *qua* party worked and made its mark as the dominant political party in the western world in the last century.

Index

M

MacGahey, Mick 108
Macleod, Iain 29, 52, 97
Macmillan, Harold 6, 7, 17, 24, 25, 34, 38–9, 43, 44, 45, 47, 77, 134
Major, John 20, 155
Mansholt, Sicco 41
Maude, Angus 52
Maudling, Reginald 48, 49, 52, 113, 115
Monnet, Jean 38

N

Nixon, Richard 75, 76–7, 78, 89

P

Patten, Chris 8
Pompidou, Georges 78, 80–1, 82, 84, 85, 86–90
Powell, Enoch 29, 31, 49, 52, 56, 62, 84, 126, 128, 133–43
Prescott, John 57
Prior, James 59

R

Rothschild, Victor 120–2

S

Soames, Christopher 80–1, 149
Straw, Jack 148, 154–5
Swinton, Lord 20

T

Thatcher, Margaret 14, 53–4, 71, 74, 79, 119, 129–31, 143, 149–50
Thorpe, Jeremy 126

W

Waldegrave, William 127, 152
Whitelaw, William 115
Wilberforce, Lord 105
Wilson, Harold 1, 5, 19, 42, 50, 53, 55, 59, 60, 61, 62, 63, 91, 92, 112, 129, 142